"Stephen Yuille offers a wonderful theological exposition of one of the most important books in the Bible. His commentary is extremely well-laid out and eminently readable. His rhetorical elegance is on display. Chock-full of insights, his exegesis is thoughtful and practical, and represents a balanced blend of biblical, systematic, and spiritual theology."

Wayne Baxter
Associate Professor of New Testament and Greek,
Heritage College & Seminary, Cambridge, ON

"In a concise, clear, and potent manner, Dr. Stephen Yuille weaves together sound exegesis, historical theology, systematic theology, and biblical theology to unpack Paul's letter to the Galatians. Adopting an expositional flavour with memorable and appropriate illustrations, reminiscent of the Puritans he is immersed in, I was not only helped to understand the content and flow of the letter, but was strengthened to quell the ever lurking legalist that slinks about in my own heart. As such, I would heartily commend this volume to every Christian and would happily put this into the hands of brothers and sisters in the congregation where I serve. Take up and read, for in doing so I expect by God's grace you will delight ever more in the blessed Trinity and the gospel of our Lord Jesus Christ."

Sean Sheeran
Pastor, Hespeler Baptist Church, Cambridge, ON

"Dr. Yuille has blessed the church with a much-needed, pastoral volume on Galatians. The strength of this work is found in the illuminating insight and excellent application to the Christian life. Each chapter is written succinctly and enables the reader to walk through Galatians devotionally. In this book, Christians will be joyfully reminded of the sole sufficiency of Christ for salvation."

Joel Kindberg
Pastor, Grace Covenant Church, Weatherford, TX

THE FULLNESS OF TIME

For the staff and faculty of Heritage College & Seminary

THE FULLNESS OF TIME

Paul's Epistle to the Galatians

J. STEPHEN YUILLE

The Fullness of Time

Copyright © 2022 J. Stephen Yuille

Unless otherwise indicated, all Scripture quotations are from The ESV® Bible (The Holy Bible, English Standard Version®), copyright © 2001 by Crossway, a publishing ministry of Good News Publishers. Used by permission. All rights reserved.

All rights reserved. This book or any portion thereof may not be reproduced or used in any manner whatsoever without the express written permission of the publisher except for the use of brief quotations in a book review.

Published by: H&E Publishing, Peterborough, Ontario, Canada
www.hesedandemet.com

Cover design by Chance Faulkner

Paperback ISBN: 978-1-77484-080-1
Ebook ISBN: 978-1-77484-081-8

Contents

Preface 1

Introduction (1:1–10)

1. Christ Alone (1:1–5) 5
2. No Other Gospel (1:6–10) 13

Section 1: The Gospel "Revealed" (1:11–2:14)

3. Called by Grace (1:11–24) 21
4. The Truth of the Gospel (2:1–14) 29

Section 2: The Gospel "Explained" (2:15–21)

5. Justified in Christ (2:15–21) 39
6. Crucified with Christ (2:15–21) 47

Section 3: The Gospel "Defended" (3:1–5:12)

7. The Gift of the Holy Spirit (3:1–5) 55
8. The Blessing of Abraham (3:6–14) 63
9. The Priority of Abraham (3:15–26) 69
10. Baptized into Christ (3:27–29) 75
11. The Offspring of Abraham (4:1–7) 81
12. A Triune Being (4:4–7) 87
13. "Born of a Woman" (4:4) 93
14. Known by God (4:8–20) 99
15. Two Sons (4:21–31) 107
16. The Offense of the Cross (5:1–12) 113

Section 4: The Gospel "Applied" (5:13–6:10)

17. Called to Freedom (5:13–15) 121
18. Walking by the Spirit (5:16–17) 127
19. Keeping in Step with the Spirit (5:18–25) 133
20. The Fruit of the Spirit in Action: Avoiding Conceit (5:26) 139
21. The Fruit of the Spirit in Action: Bearing Burdens (6:1–5) 145
22. The Fruit of the Spirit in Action: Doing Good (6:6–10) 151

Conclusion

23. Lasting Impressions (6:11–18) 159

About the Author 165
Bibliography 167
Scripture Index 173

Preface

According to Alister McGrath, "spirituality is the outworking in real life of a person's religious faith"—that is, what we do with what we believe.[1] One of the most helpful places for establishing a biblical framework for spirituality is Paul's Epistle to the Galatians. Here we're introduced to both the creed and conduct of those "who are spiritual" (Gal. 6:1).

I first preached through this epistle between June 2017 and February 2018 at Grace Community Church in Glen Rose, Texas. I've returned to it on multiple occasions since then, and I continue to find Paul's pastoral passion and doctrinal precision to be compelling, comforting, and challenging. In the pages that follow I seek to impart to you something of what I've learned.

For a detailed analysis of the epistle, the reader should consult the various commentaries. (I especially recommend Dr. Thomas Schreiner's work.) While I've done the heavy lifting of exegesis, I've limited what I share of it in this book, as my primary aim is to give "the sense" of the text while focusing on its application. I trust what lies within these pages will prove beneficial to you. I've done my best according to the gifts God has given me. As always, may he bless what's his and forgive the rest!

Deus Pro Nobis

---

[1] Alister E. McGrath, *Christian Spirituality: An Introduction* (Oxford: Blackwell Publishers, 1999), 2.

Introduction (1:1–10)

1
Christ Alone (1:1-5)

Centuries ago, Martin Luther declared, "God accepts only the forsaken, cures only the sick, gives sight only to the blind, restores life only to the dead, sanctifies only sinners, gives wisdom only to the unwise. In short, he has mercy only on those who are wretched."[1] Luther's point was well made. "I have not come to call the righteous," declares Christ, "but sinners to repentance" (Luke 5:32). In other words, the gospel is only for those who acknowledge their sin. The reason is straightforward: we won't rest in Christ alone until we're convinced of our need for Christ alone.

The Reformation was in many ways a struggle for this truth. The Roman Catholic Church affirmed that salvation is by grace *and* works; furthermore, it pointed people to Christ *and* saints, masses, pilgrimages, penances, and indulgences, as the way to obtain favour with God. In sharp contrast, the Reformers affirmed that salvation is by grace *alone* through faith *alone* in Christ *alone*. They were convinced, in the words of John Calvin, "that our whole salvation is found in Christ," and that we must, therefore, "drink our fill from this fountain and from no other."[2]

As we embark on this study of Paul's Epistle to the Galatians, my prayer is that we will indeed follow Calvin's counsel and delight in the unshakeable certainty that Christ is a sufficient Saviour.

Paul engages in three missionary journeys as recorded in Acts 13-21. Around AD 45, he departs from the city of Antioch in Syria, and sails to Cyprus. Having traversed the island, he sails to the south coast of Asia Minor (modern-day Turkey). Once there, he walks in-land, visiting the cities of Antioch, Lystra, Iconium, and Derbe—all located in Galatia.[3] He then returns home to Antioch in Syria. A few years later, he sets out for a second time. He

---

[1] Martin Luther, *Luther's Works*, 55 vols (Philadelphia: Fortress Press, 1957), 14:163.
[2] John Calvin, *Institutes of the Christian Religion*, in *The Library of Christian Classics*, vols 20-21, ed. J.T. McNeill (Philadelphia: Westminster Press, 1960), 2:16:19.
[3] There is some discussion as to which geographical region Paul means by "Galatia." I believe he's speaking of the southern part of the Roman province known as Asia Minor. See the various commentaries on Paul's Epistle to the Galatians for additional information.

travels overland to Galatia, where he visits the churches which he had established on his first journey. He proceeds into Macedonia and Greece, before returning home to Antioch. Around AD 52, he sets out for a third time. He covers a wide area, including Galatia, before ending up in Jerusalem, where he's arrested and eventually escorted as a prisoner to Rome.

On his first journey through Galatia, Paul's evangelistic work gets off to a promising start. The Word is spreading, churches are increasing, and believers are growing (Acts 13:49; 14:21; 16:5), but there's trouble on the horizon. In his absence, opponents infiltrate the churches and seek to undermine his ministry; as a result, the new converts begin to have second thoughts about Paul. They raise questions concerning the authority of his mission and the accuracy of his message. Troubled by this overt threat to the gospel, Paul writes them a letter.

Paul's first goal in writing is to defend *the authority of his mission*. He knows what his opponents are saying about him. They deny (or, at the very least, belittle) his apostolic authority. "Why should we listen to Paul? He has no more authority than anyone else." Paul responds by reminding the Galatian churches that he's an apostle, "not from men nor through man, but through Jesus Christ and God the Father, who raised him from the dead" (1:1). Here Paul makes two noteworthy assertions. (1) He didn't receive his apostleship "from men"; moreover, no one commissioned him to preach, and no one communicated to him what to preach. (2) He received his commission directly "through Jesus Christ and God the Father, who raised him from the dead." Paul seems to be drawing attention to the fact that the other apostles were called by Christ in his state of humiliation (on earth), whereas he was called by Christ in his state of exaltation (in heaven).[4]

In the New Testament (NT), the term "apostle" is used in two distinct ways. First, it's used in an *unofficial* sense; an apostle is simply a messenger (John 13:16; 2 Cor. 8:3; Phil. 2:25). That's why gospel preachers are occasionally described as "apostles" (Acts 14:4). Second, it's used in an *official* sense; an apostle is a commissioned representative of Christ. "As the Father has sent me," declared Christ to his apostles, "even so I am sending you" (John 20:21). Because he appointed them as an extension of his ministry, they possessed divine authority. That's why Paul could confidently write:

---

[4] I am indebted to William Perkins for this observation. See William Perkins, *Commentary on Galatians*, in *The Works of William Perkins*, 10 vols (Grand Rapids: Reformation Heritage Books, 2015), 2:14.

"When you received the word of God, which you heard from us, you accepted it not as the word of men but as what it really is, the word of God" (1 Thess. 2:13).

In our text, Paul uses the term "apostle" in this second sense. His aim is to remind the Galatian believers of his divine calling, while silencing those who want to undermine his authority.

Paul's second goal in writing is to defend *the accuracy of his message.* He's aware that his opponents are trying to undermine his preaching by denying the sole sufficiency of Christ in salvation. They've added to his message of "Christ alone" by insisting that salvation depends upon Christ plus human effort—specifically, observance of the Old Testament (OT) law. And so, at the outset of his letter, Paul reminds them that "grace" and "peace" come "from God our Father and the Lord Jesus Christ" (1:3).[5] This is particularly relevant to the situation that plagues the Galatian churches. They're in danger of accepting a gospel that undermines God's grace by detracting from Christ's sole sufficiency.

The fundamental question, therefore, that Paul wants to resolve for the Galatians is this: How do we receive the "grace" and "peace" that come from "God our Father and the Lord Jesus Christ"? In a wonderfully worded declaration, he grounds his answer in a historical event: Christ "gave himself for our sins to deliver us from the present evil age, according to the will of our God and Father" (1:4). Paul packs four crucial details into this single verse.

Christ "gave himself"

This statement is true in several ways: Christ gave himself in becoming a man, taking the form of a servant, living in a fallen world, ministering to those in need, enduring man's opposition, resisting Satan's temptation, and suffering mistreatment. But far eclipsing all these, he "gave himself" by dying on the cross. As he suffered an agonizing death, he didn't hurl screams of rage toward the heavens or threats of defiance toward the crowds. He didn't utter sobs of self-pity. He didn't claim his rights or promote his interests. He didn't even consider himself. Rather, he "gave himself." "For the joy that was set before him he endured the cross, despising the shame" (Heb. 12:2).

---

[5] See Romans 5:1-2.

Christ "gave himself for our sins"

Here we see why Christ gave himself—namely, "for our sins."[6] This expression points back to the sin offering in the OT (Lev. 5:11; Num. 8:8). Elsewhere, Paul says that "Christ loved us and gave himself up for us, a fragrant offering and sacrifice to God" (Eph. 5:2). Such love merits careful consideration.

(1) The *object* of his love: "Christ loved us." Because of our sin, we deserve his severity, not his mercy; we deserve his judgment, not his forgiveness; we deserve his wrath, not his love. "But God shows his love for us in that while we were still sinners, Christ died for us" (Rom. 5:8).

(2) The *measure* of his love: Christ "gave himself up for us." He exchanged wealth for poverty, majesty for humility, a throne for a manger, and a crown of glory for a crown of thorns. He did all this "for us."

(3) The *purpose* of his love: Christ gave himself up for us as "a sacrifice to God." All the OT sacrifices pointed to Christ who willingly offered himself in our place. In bearing God's wrath, he frees us from the penalty of our sin.

(4) The *result* of his love: Christ gave himself for us as "a fragrant offering to God." After the flood, Noah presented a sacrifice. We read that it was a "fragrant aroma" to God. In response, God said, "I will never again curse the ground because of man" (Gen. 8:21). That's precisely Paul's point. Christ gave himself as a "fragrant offering" to God, meaning it was pleasing to him.

In this verse, Paul leaves no doubt that the procuring price of our salvation is Christ's atoning work. It alone is sufficient to pay the penalty for our sins and satisfy God's offended justice. This ought to cure the Galatians (and us) of any notion that we can add anything to the sole sufficiency of Christ. As Martin Luther declares, "These words *[i.e., Christ gave himself for our sins]* are very thunderclaps from heaven against all kinds of self-righteousness."[7]

Christ "gave himself to deliver us from the present evil age"

In simple terms, a Christian is someone who has been delivered.[8] The term "deliver" or "rescue" is found three times in the Book of Acts. (1) "I have

---

[6] For a similar expression, see Romans 8:3; Hebrews 10:26; 13:11; 1 Peter 3:18; 1 John 4:10.
[7] Martin Luther, *A Commentary on St Paul's Epistle to the Galatians* (Cambridge: James Clarke, 1953), 47.
[8] See 1 Timothy 2:6; Titus 2:14.

surely seen the affliction of my people who are in Egypt, and have heard their groaning, and I have come down to *deliver* them" (Acts 7:34). (2) "When Peter came to himself, he said, 'Now I am sure that the Lord has sent his angel and *rescued* me from the hand of Herod and from all that the Jewish people were expecting'" (Acts 12:11). (3) "This man was seized by the Jews and was about to be killed by them when I came upon them with the soldiers and *rescued* him" (Acts 23:27).

To be rescued is to be delivered from danger. If we see someone in danger of drowning, we don't throw him a book on how to swim. It won't help him. If someone needs rescuing, it's because he's in danger and incapable of helping himself. That was our condition as we languished in bondage to sin. Thankfully, Christ rescues us from the present evil age. As Paul makes clear, there are two ages: "this age" (night) and "the age to come" (day) (Eph. 1:21; Rom. 13:12). The "present age" began at the fall and continues to the consummation. It's the fallen creation (the old humanity in Adam). The "age to come" was inaugurated at Christ's first coming and will be consummated at his second coming. It "does not begin at the conclusion of all things but in the middle of history."[9] It's the renewed creation (the new humanity in Christ). The present age is "evil" because sin permeates it, but Christ rescues us from it, and we now belong to the age to come. As a result, we're no longer enslaved to the pride, greed, anger, pessimism, darkness, rebellion, selfishness, and foolishness that mark this present age.

Elsewhere, Paul declares that "the present time has grown very short," that "the present form of this world is passing away," and that "the end of the ages has come [upon us]" (1 Cor. 7:29, 31; 10:11). By "short," Paul means *limited*. He's saying that the time between Christ's two advents is restricted, meaning it won't continue forever. The eternal kingdom is about to break into time and, when it does, it will usher in the consummation. But we're assured that Christ has delivered us "from the present evil age"—both its present bondage and future destruction.

Christ "gave himself according to the will of our God and Father"
This is a wonderful way of saying that Christ's atoning work at Calvary's cross was God's eternal plan. "He made me a polished arrow; in his quiver he hid me" (Isa. 49:2). Here Christ (the Servant of God) makes a distinction

---

[9] J.V. Fesko, *Galatians*, in *The Lectio Continua Series* (Powder Springs: Tolle Lege Press, 2012), xxvii.

between common arrows and "polished" arrows. A polished arrow is given extra care and attention. It's hidden away for a special day and special use. This is how God cherishes his Servant (Isa. 42:1). He keeps him for just the right moment—what Paul calls "the fullness of time" (4:4). And then, he sets him in his bow, and releases him to accomplish his design.

There was nothing compelling in us that caused God to send his Son. He wasn't motivated by something good, worthy, or honourable in us. He wasn't stirred by something loveable in us. Because of his sovereign grace, he willingly sent his Son to give himself for us. For this reason, we echo Paul's cry: "To him be glory for ever and ever. Amen" (1:5).

Conclusion

Paul has thus identified his two main goals in writing: (1) to defend the authority of his ministry, and (2) to defend the accuracy of his message. As J.B. Lightfoot observes, these "two threads which run through this epistle ... are knotted together in the opening salutation."[10] Central to Paul's defense is his insistence that God's "grace" and "peace" come through Christ alone.

Regrettably, an increasing number of evangelicals question this. A recent survey revealed that two-thirds of evangelical teens are comfortable with the following statement: "Christians, Jews, Muslims, Buddhists, and others all pray to the same God, even though they use different names for that God."[11] But such a notion of a "Christ-less" approach to God stands in clear opposition to the testimony of Scripture. Because of our sin, we're cut off from God. Yet Christ—fully God and fully man—bridges the expanse. He who made all things was carried in the womb of a woman, and he who upholds all things was held in the arms of a woman. He clothed himself with our humanity—body and soul. He "gave himself for our sins to deliver us from the present evil age, according to the will of our God and Father" (1:4). And he did all this as our Mediator. Having become one with him through faith, we've been "called into the fellowship of [God's] Son, Jesus Christ our Lord" (1 Cor. 1:9). We now enjoy communion with him in his names and titles; we enjoy communion with him in his righteousness and holiness; we enjoy communion with him in his death and resurrection.

---

[10] J.B. Lightfoot, *The Epistle of St. Paul to the Galatians*, in *Classic Commentary Library* (Grand Rapids: Zondervan, 1957), 71.

[11] George Barna, *Third Millennium Teens* (Ventura: The Barna Research Group, 1999), 48.

This makes "Christ alone" the sweetest truth known to man. It's the difference between feast and famine, fullness and emptiness, an eternity of joy and an eternity of sorrow. And it's the reason we heartily confess: "There is one God, and there is one mediator between God and men, the man Christ Jesus" (1 Tim. 2:5).

> The perfect righteousness of God
> is witnessed in the Saviour's blood;
> 'Tis in the cross of Christ we trace
> his righteousness, yet wondrous grace.
>
> God could not pass the sinner by,
> his sin demands that he must die;
> But in the cross of Christ we see
> how God can save us righteously.
>
> The sin is on the Saviour laid,
> 'Twas in his blood sin's debt is paid;
> Stern justice can demand no more,
> and mercy can dispense her store.
>
> The sinner who believes is free,
> can say: "The Saviour died for me;"
> can point to the atoning blood,
> and say: "This made my peace with God."[12]

---

[12] Albert Midlane, "The Perfect Righteousness of God" (hymn).

2
No Other Gospel (1:6–10)

How can sinners be righteous in God's sight? Is there a more important question than this? The answer is by grace *alone* through faith *alone* in Christ *alone*. In a word, Christ does it all. He achieves righteousness in his obedience, and he satisfies God's offended justice by his death upon the cross. The implication is that we're completely passive. We simply receive Christ through faith and, as a result, "we become the righteousness of God in him" (2 Cor. 5:21). Our faith pays nothing, merits nothing, and contributes nothing. That's exceedingly good news!

But what happens if we add something to this good news? Intentionally or not, we end up denying the sole sufficiency of Christ. "What this means in practice is spelled out in what we can call ... theological mathematics. ... whenever you add, you subtract. Adding more to the Lord Jesus makes him less than he should be. Whenever you put a plus sign after Jesus, you are taking something away from his supremacy and sufficiency."[1] And this is what makes Paul's Epistle to the Galatians so important. He confronts those who subtract from Christ by adding to the gospel.

When studying a book of the Bible, it's important to establish the author's purpose in writing. As we noted in the last chapter, Paul writes this letter to defend the authority of his mission and the accuracy of his message. It's also important, at the outset, to map out how the author accomplishes his purpose. With that in mind, here's a very simple outline of Paul's thought-flow:

Salutation (1:1–5)
Caution (1:6–10)

Paul defends the authority of his mission:
    (1) The Gospel "Revealed" (1:11–2:14)

---

[1] Allan Chapple, *True Devotion: In Search of Authentic Spirituality* (London: The Latimer Trust, 2014), 31.

(2) The Gospel "Explained" (2:15–21)
Paul defends the accuracy of his message:
  (3) The Gospel "Defended" (3:1–5:12)
  (4) The Gospel "Applied" (4:13–6:10)

Caution (6:11–17)
Benediction (6:18)

We've considered Paul's salutation (1:1–5); now we come to his word of caution (1:6–10). The first thing to notice is what he doesn't include in these verses. In his other letters, Paul always begins by greeting his readers and then thanking God for them.[2] But there's no word of thanksgiving in the opening of this letter. Instead, Paul expresses bewilderment at the Galatian churches. "I am astonished," he declares (1:6). Why? They're "deserting" Christ. The term "desert" means "to bring to another place." Metaphorically, it describes someone who has changed allegiance; that is, switched sides amid an armed conflict. It would be like Admiral Lord Nelson joining the French, or General George Patton joining the Germans. Why is the Galatians' desertion of Christ so astonishing?

The quickness of their desertion (1:6)

Paul says he's "astonished" that they're "so quickly deserting" Christ. The expression "so quickly" echoes an incident in Israel's history.[3] God pours out ten plagues on Egypt, delivers Israel from slavery, divides the waters of the sea, and manifests his glory at Sinai. Then, Moses ascends the mountain to receive the law. But what happens? In his absence, the Israelites prostrate themselves before a golden calf. God declares to Moses: "Go down … They have turned aside *quickly* out of the way that I commanded them" (Exod. 32:8).

We see the same thing in the case of the Galatians. Upon reading Acts 13–14, we discover that Paul's initial foray into the region is successful. Because of opposition, he needs to flee for his life on a couple of occasions, but he still manages to establish churches and appoints elders, and the work is

---

[2] See Romans 1:8; 1 Corinthians 1:4; Ephesians 1:16; Philippians 1:3; Colossians 1:3; 1 Thessalonians 1:2; 2 Thessalonians 1:3.

[3] I am indebted to Thomas Schreiner for this observation. See Thomas Schreiner, *Galatians: Exegetical Commentary on the New Testament* (Grand Rapids: Zondervan, 2010), 85.

flourishing as a result. In a relatively short period of time, however, these new converts are calling into question both Paul's ministry and message. It's as though they've completely forgotten what had happened but a brief time ago. In a word, it's astonishing.

The seriousness of their desertion (1:6)
Paul says they're deserting "him who called [them] in the grace of Christ and are turning to a different gospel." The full import of Paul's concern becomes evident when we work backwards through this verse and note a three-fold progression in their desertion.

First, they're deserting the gospel. The false teachers in their midst are proclaiming "a different gospel." It isn't really a different gospel, as there's only one gospel, which Paul highlights in his salutation (1:1-5). In sum, grace and peace come through Christ who gave himself for our sins to deliver us from the present evil age, according to the will of God. This means that God is gracious to sinners for Christ's sake. But the false teachers have added to the gospel whereby it's no longer a divine gift but a human achievement.

Second, they're deserting the grace of Christ. Any addition to the gospel is ultimately a repudiation of Christ's sufficiency. If we add a drop of poison to a healthy beverage, what happens? It's ruined. Similarly, if we add anything to Christ, we ruin the gospel. As Paul declares later in this epistle, "You are severed from Christ, you who would be justified by the law; you have fallen away from grace" (5:4).

Third, they're deserting God—the One who called them (1:15; 5:8).[4] This means that their rejection of the gospel is ultimately a rejection of God.

The cause of their desertion (1:7)
The reason for their desertion is abundantly clear: "There are some who trouble you and want to distort the gospel of Christ." They "distort" the gospel by twisting it into something it isn't. Here's what they might have sounded like in Paul's day:

> Dear brothers in Galatia. We've heard of what God has accomplished among you through Paul. You've turned from paganism. You've turned from idolatry. You've turned to the living God through his

---

[4] See Romans 8:30; 1 Corinthians 1:9, 26; Ephesians 4:1; Colossians 3:15; 1 Thessalonians 4:7; 1 Timothy 6:12.

Son, Jesus Christ. This is wonderful! But we want to inform you that Paul's teaching is deficient in a couple of ways. Our main issue is with what he doesn't say. He isn't preaching the full gospel. Has he spoken to you of the need for circumcision? Has he spoken to you of the importance of the Mosaic Law? We doubt it. We've noticed he's weak in these areas. And yet, your observance of these things is necessary if you wish to be a part of the new Israel. This is the gospel in its fullness, and this is the gospel we preach. We pray God will open your eyes to see the truth of what we're saying.

By distorting the gospel, these men "trouble" the churches of Galatia.[5] The term "trouble" is *tarasso*, which means to agitate. Years ago, I was preaching at a Bible conference in Kilkenny, Ireland. Alison (my wife) and I were staying with friends who had two young girls. One morning, a group of us went for a walk in the countryside. It was everything I'd imagined Ireland to be—lush green fields, old stone houses, narrow windy roads, gently falling drizzle. It was peaceful and beautiful. As we crossed over a small pond by way of a footbridge, one of the girls threw an enormous rock into the water. After the initial splash, the ripples quickly spread to the banks of the pond. In a word, the water was agitated. This is precisely what the false teachers among the Galatians are doing. They're troubling (agitating) the churches by attacking Paul's credibility and disparaging the gospel he preaches.

These two (troubling and distorting) always go together. John Stott observes,

> To tamper with the gospel is always to trouble the church. You cannot touch the gospel and leave the church untouched, because the church is created and lives by the gospel. Indeed, the church's greatest troublemakers (now as then) are not those outside who oppose, ridicule, and persecute it, but those inside who try to change the gospel.[6]

Today, the greatest "agitators" are still those who undermine the sole sufficiency of Christ.

---

[5] See Acts 15:24.
[6] John Stott, *The Message of Galatians*, in *The Bible Speaks Today* (Downers Grove: InterVarsity Press, 1968), 23.

The result of their desertion (1:8-9)
Paul declares that anyone who preaches "a different gospel," and by implication anyone who believes it, is to be "accursed." There are two schools of thought as to his meaning.

First, Paul might be referring to their standing before true believers. Simply put, we're to reject those who distort the gospel.[7] This isn't an excuse to be rude or belligerent. It's simply a warning to stop listening to them and to treat them as unbelievers.

Second, Paul might be referring to their standing before God. For what it's worth, I'm inclined to this interpretation. To desert the gospel is to turn one's back on God's grace in Christ. What's left? The consequence for believing anything but the gospel is judgment. It's to hear God say: "Depart from me, for I never knew you" (Matt. 7:23). To be cursed is to lose God—the only source of true happiness. It's a loss that no words can describe, and no mind can conceive. The "accursed" are the object of divine wrath, as God hides his love and mercy.

Conclusion
Paul uses some very strong language in these verses. He rebukes the Galatians for their "desertion" of Christ, he laments their "distortion" of the gospel, and he declares that all who hold a different gospel are "accursed." Perhaps wanting to soften the blow, he adds, "For am I now seeking the approval of man, or of God? Or am I trying to please man? If I were still trying to please man, I would not be a servant of Christ" (1:10). Here Paul reminds his readers that he isn't a man-pleaser. If his goal were to secure the favour of his fellow Jews, then he wouldn't be a servant of Christ. Obviously, he hasn't chosen the path to worldly fame and honour. He has chosen to serve Christ, and he serves Christ by proclaiming the gospel—namely, that we're only reconciled to God through Christ, and we only receive Christ through faith.

Are we convinced like Paul of the sole sufficiency of Christ? Are we convinced that Christ offered himself upon the cross to make atonement for sin? He became one with us in our humanity. "He stripped himself of the robes of his glory and covered himself with the rags of our humanity."[8] Because he's related to us, he can act as our Redeemer. He's able to pay our debt and pur-

---

[7] See Matthew 7:15; Acts 20:28-29; Romans 16:17; Philippians 3:2, 18; 2 Timothy 3:5; 2 John 10-11.

[8] Thomas Watson, *A Body of Divinity* (Edinburgh: Banner of Truth, 1958), 196-198.

chase our inheritance. "Christ was delivered up for our trespasses and raised for our justification" (Rom. 4:25). He paid the penalty for our sin on the cross, and God testified to his acceptance of Christ's sacrifice by raising him from the dead. Christ's work, therefore, is enough to atone for our sin, to secure God's forgiveness, and to reconcile us to God. "For Christ also suffered once for sins, the just for the unjust, that he might bring us to God" (1 Pet. 3:18).

Are we convinced that God offers Christ to sinners for their salvation? We don't need to fulfill any conditions. We don't need to get our act together. We don't need to meet a certain standard of behaviour. We don't need to be sorry enough, ashamed enough, good enough, or holy enough. We simply need to receive God's offer. In the words of Horatius Bonar, "Upon a life I did not live, upon a death I did not die, another's life, another's death, I stake my whole eternity."[9] It's important to remind ourselves of God's free offer of Christ, because a spirit of legalism lurks in each of us. Deep down, we're convinced that there's something we must do that will make the difference between heaven and hell. Yet, Paul makes it clear that "those who are in the flesh cannot please God" (Rom. 8:8). Our only hope is to look away from ourselves to Christ who has done all. The gospel isn't a work to be performed, but a message to be received.

Are we convinced that we receive God's gift (Christ) through faith? When we realize we're physically sick, we look for a doctor. Similarly, when we realize we're spiritually sick, we look for a Saviour. This means that Christ is sweet when sin is bitter. When we see our sinfulness before a holy God, we extend the hand of our soul to receive Christ as ours. Having become one with him, we take possession of all the benefits and blessings that are found in him. To be united to Christ is justification, adoption, reconciliation, and sanctification. To be united to Christ is salvation. There is no other gospel.

---

[9] Horatius Bonar, "Upon a Life I Have Not lived" (hymn).

Section 1:
The Gospel "Revealed" (1:11–2:14)

3
Called by Grace (1:11–24)

Testimonies of the power of God's grace are compelling. This is one of the reasons I enjoy reading biographies of believers from years ago—men and women like William Carey, Hudson Taylor, Adoniram Judson, George Muller, Amy Carmichael, Charles Spurgeon, and Lottie Moon. It's both encouraging and challenging to see how God worked in and through their lives.

We find a stirring testimony of the power of God's grace in 1:11–24, where Paul describes how God saved him and appointed him to preach the gospel. These verses are part of a larger section, The Gospel Revealed (1:11–2:14), in which Paul mounts a defense of his apostolic authority. His opponents allege that his gospel is from man—more specifically, that he has distorted what he received from the other apostles. Given the seriousness of the charge and its negative impact upon the churches of Galatia, Paul seeks to set the record straight.

Paul's argument stated (1:11–12)
Paul contends that he didn't "receive" the gospel from "any man" but "through a revelation of Jesus Christ." To appreciate his point, it's important to note that the term "revelation" is used in two ways in Scripture.

First, there is *extraordinary* revelation whereby the Holy Spirit teaches *immediately*—without the Word. "We impart a secret and hidden wisdom of God," says Paul, "these things God has *revealed* to us through the Spirit" (1 Cor. 2:7, 10). Here the term "us" refers to the apostles in the early church. Thus, Paul is affirming that the Holy Spirit revealed divine truths directly to them. This revelation constitutes "the faith" (i.e., the body of revealed truth) which "was once for all delivered to the saints" (Jude 1:3).

Second, there is *ordinary* revelation whereby the Holy Spirit teaches *mediately*—with the Word. Paul prays "that the God of our Lord Jesus Christ, the Father of glory, may give you a spirit of wisdom and of *revelation* in the knowledge of him" (Eph. 1:17). This is what the Holy Spirit does when we read and hear the Bible. He reveals (or illumines) what he has inspired (Scripture), so that we can understand it and apply it.

In our text, Paul is speaking of the first—extraordinary revelation. His point is that he received his gospel directly from God; thus, contrary to what his opponents contend, his gospel is most certainly divine (not human) in origin.

Paul's argument defended (1:13-2:14)

Why should anyone believe Paul's assertion that he received his gospel by way of divine revelation as opposed to human instruction? He furnishes four reasons.

First, he appeals to his *conversion* to Christ (1:13-15). Here he's addressing those who say, "Paul's gospel is man-made." He shows that this accusation is nonsense. There was a time when he was "advancing in Judaism" and he was zealous for the "traditions of the fathers." He was even a violent persecutor of the church. But God converted him, and now he preaches the very thing he formerly despised. The suggestion, therefore, that his gospel is man-made is unfounded.

Second, Paul appeals to his *seclusion* from the other apostles (1:16-24). Here he's countering those who say, "Paul received the gospel from the apostles at Jerusalem." He carefully demonstrates the absurdity of this assertion by showing that he had spent relatively little time with the other apostles. After his conversion, he preached in Damascus before moving to Arabia for three years; then he returned to Damascus. When he finally visited Jerusalem (Acts 9:26-30), he saw Peter and James, but he wasn't with them for more than a couple of weeks. After this visit, he proceeded to the regions of Cilicia and Syria. The suggestion, therefore, that he received his gospel from the other apostles is baseless.

Third, Paul appeals to his *confirmation* by the other apostles (2:1-10). In making this appeal, he has in view those who say, "Paul has altered the gospel." To refute this charge, he again appeals to the historical record. After fourteen years, he visited Jerusalem for a second time.[1] Peter, James, and

---

[1] Is Acts 11:27-30 or 15:1-2 in view? See the various commentaries on Paul's Epistle to the Galatians for the different theories as to when this visit occurred.

John welcomed him.[2] They didn't take any issue with the content of his gospel. No one contradicted his teaching that justification is by grace alone through faith alone in Christ alone. The suggestion, therefore, that he altered the gospel is without factual support.

Fourth, Paul appeals to his *confrontation* of the apostle Peter (2:11-14). Here he refutes those who say, "Paul isn't a real apostle." Yet again, the accusation contradicts the facts. At Antioch in Syria, some of the Jews had insisted that the observance of the OT law was necessary for salvation. Out of fear, Peter followed them in their error. But Paul took a stand, openly challenging his fellow apostle. The logical inference is that Peter subsequently repented of his error. The suggestion, therefore, that Paul isn't a real apostle is unconvincing.

And that's how Paul's argument unfolds in 1:11-2:14. Focusing for a moment on 1:13-24, it's worth noting the wonderful display of the riches of God's grace in Paul's personal testimony.

Distinguishing grace
By Paul's own confession, there was a time when he was "advancing in Judaism" and was extremely "zealous" for the traditions of the fathers (1:14). This zeal led him to persecute the church and attempt to destroy it (1:13). Undoubtedly, he thought he was a modern-day Phinehas, who was "jealous with [the LORD's] jealousy" and killed those who dared to violate the law (Num. 25:11). Or perhaps he thought he was acting like Elijah, who was "very jealous for the LORD" and killed the prophets of Baal (1 Kgs. 19:10-14). Paul probably saw these men as expressions of deep piety, but his zeal for religion was merely an external façade far removed from any true knowledge of God (Rom. 10:2). All that to say, Paul was completely lost. But what happened? In his own words, "he who had set me apart before I was born, and who called me by his grace, was pleased to reveal his Son to me" (1:15-16). Here Paul mentions three defining moments on his path to salvation.

First, God set Paul apart before he was born.[3] This is known as the doctrine of election. As Paul says elsewhere, "God chose you as the firstfruits to be saved, through sanctification by the Spirit and belief in the truth" (2

---

[2] J.V. Fesko explains that Paul's description of these men as "pillars" (2:9) is an illusion to the pillars in Solomon's temple (1 Kgs. 7:15-22) and, therefore, a declaration that the church is the final temple. See Fesko, *Galatians*, 26-27.

[3] In his choice of words (1:13) Paul is likely comparing his calling to that of the OT prophets (Isa. 49:1-6; Jer. 1:5).

Thess. 2:13). "Here we have the Holy Spirit's pre-conversion work," writes William MacDonald. "He sets individuals apart to God from the world, convicts them of sin, and points them to Christ. Someone has well said: 'If it had not been for Christ, there would have been no *feast*; if it had not been for the Holy Spirit, there would have been no *guests*.'"[4] Interestingly, Paul doesn't say God "chose" us *because* of our "sanctification by the Spirit and belief in the truth." These aren't the causes of salvation, but simply the means through which God applies salvation. God didn't choose us so that we might believe. We believe because God chose us. This means that all good is the fruit of predestination. If it were the cause, then predestination would be post-destination.

Second, Paul says that God called him by his grace. This is the doctrine of effectual calling. Two calls are identified in Scripture. The first is the general call. It's external, meaning it's heard with the ear. It's the proclamation of God's Word by the preacher (Matt. 11:28; John 7:37; Acts 16:31). This can't be what Paul is talking about here. Why not? He makes it clear that he was "extremely zealous" in his religiosity. He wasn't seeking the truth. On the contrary, he was living in open rebellion against God. Therefore, God's call wasn't a mere invitation, but a powerful operation in Paul's heart. This brings us to the second call in Scripture: the special (or effectual) call. It's internal, meaning it's heard with the soul. It's the application of God's Word by the Spirit (Rom. 1:6–7). This was the Galatians' experience (1:6) as well as Paul's. God had called him by his grace, and he had responded in faith. As Christ declares, "Everyone who has heard and learned from the Father comes to me" (John 6:45).

Third, Paul says that God was "pleased" to reveal his Son to him. Elsewhere, he writes, "I was once alive apart from the law, but when the commandment came, sin came alive and I died" (Rom. 7:9). He had studied the law since his childhood, yet he lacked any experiential knowledge of it. Without such knowledge, he was "alive," meaning he thought all was well with his soul, and he was self-satisfied (Phil. 3:6). However, the time came when he "died." Why? The law struck home, and sin became alive, and he saw the depths of his depravity. Thankfully, God opened his eyes to the wonders of the cross, and he received Christ through faith.

---

[4] William MacDonald, *Believers Bible Commentary—New Testament* (Nashville: Thomas Nelson, 1989), 872.

CALLED BY GRACE (1:11-24)

Overflowing grace

Paul's present condition as a believer (and as an apostle of Christ) is startling, given his past condition (1:13). Elsewhere, he provides a brief description of his life before God called him, and it isn't very flattering (1 Tim. 1:13). (1) He was a "blasphemer" (one who slanders God). (2) He was a "persecutor" (one who pursues as a hunter). (3) He was a "violent aggressor" (one who deliberately mistreats others for the purpose of hurting and humiliating them). In sum, Paul was a God-hater.

But what does he go on to say? "The grace of our Lord overflowed for me" (1 Tim. 1:14). In other words, God's grace toward Paul was hyper-plentiful. Paul says the reason he "received mercy" was that Christ might "display his perfect patience as an example to those who were to believe in him for eternal life" (1 Tim. 1:16). His point is that it doesn't matter how wicked we are, God is willing to forgive. How can we be so sure? He saved Paul! His conversion is a pattern of God's abounding mercy toward the most sinful, rebellious, antagonistic, spiteful, self-centred, depraved individuals.

Can anything move us beyond the reach of God's grace? His grace overflowed for drunken Noah, idolatrous Abraham, rebellious Jacob, and murderous David. God's grace overflowed for the thief, the prostitute, the demoniac, and the publican. God's grace "overflowed" for Paul. God accepts all those who turn to him in faith and repentance. God's acceptance of Christ guarantees his acceptance of all who are united with Christ through faith. God receives us because he receives Christ; he welcomes us because he welcomes Christ; he's pleased with us because he's pleased with Christ. This is overflowing grace.

Transforming grace

Paul ends this section with these words: "They glorified God because of me!" (1:24) Who's he talking about? Paul is speaking of the churches of Judea. They'd never met him, but they knew of him. At one time, they stood in dread of him because he was a violent persecutor of the church (1:13); but now he's preaching "the faith he once tried to destroy" (1:23). And so, they glorify God for the transforming power of his grace as exemplified in Paul's life.

Elsewhere, Paul writes, "For the grace of God that brings salvation has appeared to all men, teaching us that, denying ungodliness and worldly lusts, we should live soberly, righteously, and godly in the present age (Titus 2:11-

12). Did you catch the twofold emphasis? God's grace has appeared to *save* us and *teach* us. We must never divorce the two. Because of Adam's fall, we suffer a two-fold problem: (1) *condemnation*—we've lost God's favour and fallen under the penalty of sin; and (2) *corruption*—we've lost God's image and fallen under the power of sin. But the gospel remedies both. Christ restores God's favour to us by paying the penalty for our sin, and he renews God's image in us by breaking the power of our sin. The first is called justification, while the second is called sanctification. They're the twofold fruit of union with Christ, and while distinct they're inseparable. "It is absurd to imagine that God should justify a people and not sanctify them," declares Thomas Watson.[5]

Conclusion

Most people are confused when it comes to how they perceive their relationship with God. Some think of their relationship in *positive* terms, and simply assume God loves them. Some think of their relationship in *neutral* terms, meaning they don't feel very strongly about God one way or the other. The sad fact is that no one thinks of their relationship in *negative* terms, yet that's precisely how the Bible describes it. As Paul says, we're "dead in trespasses and sins" (Eph. 2:1) and "alienated and hostile in mind" (Col. 1:21).

This wretched predicament makes "grace" a beautiful word. Because of our sin, we can't know God unless he makes himself known to us, and we can't come to God unless he calls us. The gospel is the good news that God is gracious. In the gospel he offers Christ to us. We offer nothing to him in exchange for his gift of salvation. The Father's giving of the Son for us is a gift; the Son's giving of the Spirit to us is a gift; our identity in Christ is a gift; forgiveness is a gift; adoption is a gift; glorification is a gift. This is difficult for us to appreciate because most of our earthly gifts are a response to advancements, achievements, and accomplishments. In other words, most of our earthly gifts are earned. But God's gifts are radically different. They're gracious—unearned, unmerited, and undeserved.

What a powerful reminder that our strength, knowledge, achievements, ambitions, deeds, and desires are of no merit in God's sight. As Martin Luther notes, "The doctrine of the gospel removes from mankind all glory, wisdom, righteousness, and so on and gives it solely to the Creator, who

---

[5] Quoted in I.D.E. Thomas (ed.), *A Golden Treasury* (Edinburgh: Banner of Truth, 2000), 141.

made everything out of nothing (Heb. 11:3)."[6] When it's all said and done, we have no refuge except in God's grace.

> Marvelous grace of our loving Lord,
> Grace that exceeds our sin and our guilt!
> Yonder on Calvary's mount out-poured—
> There where the blood of the Lamb was spilt.
>
> Grace, grace, God's grace,
> Grace that will pardon and cleanse within;
> Grace, grace, God's grace,
> Grace that is greater than all our sin![7]

---

[6] Luther, *Galatians*, 78.
[7] Julia H. Johnston, "Marvelous Grace of Our Loving Lord" (hymn).

4
The Truth of the Gospel (2:1–14)

When Martin Luther posted his "95 theses" on the church door in Wittenberg in 1517, he was inviting the clerical community to debate various abuses within the Roman Catholic Church. In the preface to his theses, he mentions that he was compelled to speak "out of love for the truth and the desire to bring it to light."[1] His actions propelled him into a whirlwind of controversy. Three years later, in 1520, he published three books aimed at the pillars of Roman Catholic dogma.[2] The next year, he was summoned to give an account before the emperor at a council in the city of Worms. When he was given the opportunity to recant, he refused. He was subsequently sentenced to death and granted twenty-one days to get his affairs in order. He escaped arrest but lived the rest of his life assuming each day would be his last. Luther never compromised because he was compelled by his love for God's Word. Despite his many shortcomings (yes, some glaring), he stands as a towering example of unwavering devotion to the truth of the gospel.

We're going to see similar devotion in 2:1–14. Some in the churches of Galatia are trying to discredit Paul's ministry. Their charge goes something like this:

> Paul doesn't preach the full gospel. He received the gospel from the other apostles, but he has corrupted it. He speaks of Christ's crucifixion and resurrection. He speaks of believing in Christ and confessing sin. All good! But he refuses to tell people that there's more. He fails to mention that they need to follow the OT Jewish laws, and that circumcision is necessary, abstaining from certain foods is necessary, and ceremonial washings are necessary. Paul is telling people that none of these things matter. He has altered the full gospel which he received from the other apostles. Clearly, he isn't an apostle of the same stature as them. He isn't one of the pillars of the church at Jerusalem!

---

[1] https://www.luther.de/en/95thesen.html.
[2] I.e., *The Address to the Christian Nobility of the German Nation*; *The Babylonian Captivity of the Church*; *The Freedom of a Christian*.

Because of this smear campaign, the churches of Galatia are "quickly deserting" Christ (1:6). Paul recognizes that the situation is desperate. To set the record straight, he essentially says the following:

> I would have you know that my gospel isn't man-made. I didn't receive it from anyone. I received it through a revelation of Jesus Christ. Let me remind you of four facts. The first is my *conversion* to Christ (1:11-15). The gospel is antithetical to what I was before Christ saved me. Apart from a work of God's sovereign grace, how do you explain that I now preach what I once persecuted? To suggest that my gospel is my own invention makes no sense. The second fact is my *seclusion* from the other apostles (1:16-24). After my conversion, I spent three years in Damascus and Arabia. Then, I went to Cilicia and Syria. During those years, I only spent two weeks in Jerusalem. Explain to me how I received the gospel from the other apostles when I barely know the other apostles! The third fact is my *confirmation* by the other apostles (2:1-10). When I visited Jerusalem for a second time, Peter, James, and John met with me, but they didn't take any issue with the gospel I preach. They didn't require Titus to be circumcised. They only asked me to remember the poor. If my gospel differs from what they preach, why didn't they say anything? The fourth fact is my *confrontation* of the apostle Peter (2:11-14). While at Antioch, Peter stumbled in living out the gospel. Because he was afraid of the Jews, he withdrew from eating with the Gentiles.[3] I rebuked him to his face. He knew he was wrong because he knows the gospel (as do I). These four facts prove that what my detractors are saying about my ministry is baseless, defenseless, and downright ludicrous.

In the last study, we entered the first half of Paul's testimony (1:11-24) to consider the wonder of God's sovereign grace. Now, we're going to enter the second half of his testimony (2:1-14) to consider what it means to preserve the truth of the gospel. We find this expression in 2:5, "To them we did not yield in submission even for a moment, so that the truth of the gospel might be preserved for you."

What does it mean to preserve the "truth of the gospel"? This is an important question because (as Paul demonstrates in this letter) subtle shifts to the gospel are deadly. I was reminded recently of the Challenger disaster in 1986. What caused the disintegration of the space shuttle? An O-ring seal in

---

[3] Peter had no excuse for his conduct. See Acts 10:15.

one of the boosters failed at liftoff. Something so seemingly insignificant had such a catastrophic result. The same is true when it comes to the gospel. Subtle shifts are potentially disastrous. With that in mind, here are four truths (emerging from 2:1-14) that we would do well to guard at all costs.

The gospel is God's revelation (2:2, 11)

Paul insists that he received the gospel directly from Christ (1:11-12). From what he writes in 2:1-11, it's apparent that he doesn't view the apostles (himself included) as *above* this revelation.

For starters, Paul expects the other apostles to *recognize* God's revelation. He says, "I went up [to Jerusalem] because of a revelation and set before them (though privately before those who seemed influential) the gospel that I proclaim among the Gentiles, in order to make sure I was not running or had not run in vain" (2:2). Paul doesn't visit Jerusalem, so that the other apostles can ratify his gospel. He doesn't think to himself: "Perhaps I've been wrong the past seventeen years. I better consult with the other apostles to find out." On the contrary, he visits Jerusalem because God has commanded him to do so. He sets his gospel before the other apostles, and he expects them to recognize it for what it is. If they don't, it means he has been running "in vain"—that is to say, it means he has erred in contending that they aren't Judaizers.

Secondly, Paul expects the other apostles to *follow* God's revelation. "But when Cephas came to Antioch, I opposed him to his face, because he stood condemned" (2:11). Formerly Peter (Cephas) had eaten with the Gentiles without insisting on any observance of the OT law. But now he's afraid of offending the "circumcision party" (2:12), and so he withdraws from the Gentile believers, and many (including Barnabas) follow him in his "hypocrisy" (2:13). Paul confronts Peter to his face because of his departure from the truth. It's important to note that Peter and Paul don't differ theologically. The issue is that Peter isn't living in accordance with the truth he confesses. In confronting Peter, Paul expects him to submit to the truth of the gospel (God's revelation) by changing his behaviour.

To preserve the truth of the gospel, we must embrace it as God's revelation. This is a timely reminder, given the prevalence of relativism in our day. Many people reject all notions of "metanarratives"—cohesive explanations of the world. They reject the basic premise that objective knowledge is attainable. They reject any appeal to ultimate evidence. This means that, for many people, all ideas, thoughts, and worldviews are plausible. It's into this great void that we declare the gospel. As we do, we must remember that we aren't promoting human ideas, theories, or philosophies, but proclaiming God's revelation to man. "Those who fear God stand in awe of the Word," says John Bunyan. "[They] have the very form of that Word engraved upon the face of their souls."[4]

The gospel exalts Christ as the only means of salvation (2:3, 6, 7, 10)

Paul's visit with the other apostles in Jerusalem is very informative. Please notice four details. (1) They don't compel Titus to be circumcised (2:3).[5] (2) They don't correct the content of Paul's preaching (2:6). (3) They don't withhold fellowship from him (2:9). (4) They don't require anything from him except that he minister to the poor (2:10).[6] In short, they recognize his gospel as their gospel, meaning they too are convinced that justification is by grace alone through faith alone in Christ alone.

To preserve the truth of the gospel, we must exalt Christ as the only means of salvation. Are you familiar with the phrase "the crux of the matter"? We use it to refer to the most important point. The term "crux" is Latin—the origin of our words "crucial" and "cross." In other words, the cross is crucial. The central message of the Bible is the inauguration and consummation of God's kingdom in Christ. This means the central message of the Bible is the cross. There's something intrinsic to the character of God that requires death as a payment for sin. We desperately need a mediator to stand between us and a holy God, to make atonement for sin (Rom. 3:21-26). This mediator is Christ alone. We must, therefore, be uncompromising in our exaltation of Christ as a sufficient Saviour.

> Bearing shame and scoffing rude,
> In my place condemned he stood;
> Sealed my pardon with his blood.
> Hallelujah! What a Saviour!

---

[4] John Bunyan, *A Treatise on the Fear of God* (London, 1679; rpt. Morgan: Soli Deo Gloria, 1999), 77.

[5] The rite of circumcision pointed to Christ's redeeming work. See Genesis 17:14; Isaiah 53:8; Jeremiah 11:19; Luke 12:50; Colossians 2:11.

[6] See Acts 11:29-30; 24:17; Romans 15:17; 1 Corinthians. 15:1; 2 Corinthians 8:1-15; 9:1-5.

Guilty, vile, and helpless we;
Spotless Lamb of God was he;
Full atonement! can it be?
Hallelujah! What a Saviour![7]

The gospel tears down all ethnic and cultural barriers (2:7-8)

Paul mentions that the apostles at Jerusalem recognized that he had been entrusted with "the gospel to the uncircumcised" just as Peter had been entrusted with "the gospel to the circumcised." Paul isn't speaking of two different gospels, but two different cultures in which the one gospel is preached. God sends Paul to the Gentiles and Peter to the Jews, indicating that their principal mission is to one of these two groups. Historically, this has been the most volatile of all ethnic distinctions, but it ends with Christ's coming. In him there's neither Jew nor Gentile (3:28).

To preserve the truth of the gospel, we must resist the temptation to attach our culture, country, or ethnicity to it. The gospel is multi-cultural, meaning it's for the Canadian, Italian, Kenyan, and Indian. It knows nothing of culture, social status, or political party. When we equate the gospel with our specific cultural/national identity, we invariably drift toward "another" gospel. For this reason, we must be careful to adopt Paul's mindset: "I have become all things to all people, that by all means I might save some" (1 Cor. 9:22). To those under the law (Jews), Paul became as one under the law (1 Cor. 9:20) (This doesn't mean he became a legalist). To those outside the law (Gentiles), he became as one outside the law (1 Cor. 9:21) (This doesn't mean he became a libertine). Paul's point is that he refused to allow cultural differences to become a stumbling block to his preaching of the gospel. When among Jews, he dressed and talked like Jews; when among Gentiles, he dressed and talked like Gentiles. When among Jews, he had Timothy circumcised (Acts 16:3); when among Gentiles, he didn't have Titus circumcised (Gal. 2:3-5). Paul is convinced that Christ transcends all cultural allegiance. Being a Christian is his basic identity. Therefore, he's able to adopt and drop cultural practices at a moment's notice because his identity isn't tied to these things.

This ought to be our strategy—to become all things to all people so that we might win some for Christ. It doesn't mean we compromise the truth in the name of cultural relevance, nor does it mean we engage in cultural prac-

---

[7] Phillip Paul Bliss, "Man of Sorrows, What a Name" (hymn).

tices that are contrary to God's Word. It simply means that we don't confuse cultural preferences with the gospel, and we don't allow cultural differences to become stumbling blocks to the gospel.

The gospel brings freedom (2:4)

Paul reminds the Galatian churches of the "freedom" that believers have "in Christ Jesus." This is the case because Christ has fulfilled the law: he meets its requirement and pays its penalty. The implication is obvious: to be without Christ is to be obligated to meet a requirement we can't meet and to pay a penalty we can't pay. That's bondage. But to be in Christ is to enjoy freedom. Thomas Schreiner explains, "Those who live under the old age of the law are enslaved, whereas those who are in Christ live in the new era in which God's saving promises are being fulfilled."[8]

To preserve the truth of the gospel, we must not "yield" to those who would undermine "the freedom we have in Christ Jesus." Anything that detracts from the sole sufficiency of Christ is to be vigorously rejected. Have you ever seen the finish to a marathon? Many of the athletes collapse at the end of the race because they're completely exhausted—every ounce of their energy is spent. That's how we feel when we understand the law. It requires us to do something we can't do, thereby humbling us for our sin. Having learned the disease of our spiritual inability, we begin to yearn for Christ and his merits. We hunger and thirst after a righteousness that isn't our own—"the righteousness of God without the law" (Rom. 3:21). We take to heart Paul's admonition: "Whoever calls on the name of the Lord shall be saved" (Rom. 10:13). We recognize that Christ lived the life we were required to live, and he died the death we were condemned to die. In Christ, we now possess all the perfection we need to please God, all the righteousness we need to stand before God, and all the obedience we need to be accepted by God. We rest in Christ. Our exhaustion is removed in him, our weariness is removed in him, and our burden is removed in him. This is freedom indeed!

Conclusion

I recall visiting a boy in the hospital, some years ago, who was struggling with a severe asthma attack. He was breathing through a mask connected to a nebulizer, which was getting albuterol (or something like that) deep into his

---

[8] Schreiner, *Galatians*, 125.

lungs to ease the constriction. It didn't look very comfortable, but he never thought about taking it off. Why? It was life. Similarly, the gospel is life. When condemned sinners come to Christ through faith, they find an all-sufficient Saviour. They won't part with him for all the world has to offer. They won't let go of "the truth of the gospel" (2:5).

Section 2:
The Gospel "Explained" (2:15–21)

5
Justified in Christ (2:15-21)

By the fourteenth century, the Roman Catholic Church affirmed that man co-operates with God's grace in salvation; more specifically, that faith and works lead to justification. Martin Luther, in many ways the catalyst of the Reformation, opposed Rome's teaching. He proclaimed and defended the doctrine of justification by grace alone through faith alone in Christ alone. "It is most necessary," says Luther, "that we should know this article well, teach it unto others, and beat it into their heads continually."[1] That's my aim in this study.

In 2:15-21, we find one of the most lucid explanations of the doctrine of justification that's found in all of Scripture. As one scholar observes, "The whole paragraph is in fact the arena where some of the most fundamental questions of Pauline theology have to be fought."[2] It constitutes the second major section in the flow of Paul's letter:

Salutation (1:1-5)
Caution (1:6-10)

Paul defends the authority of his mission:
    (1) The Gospel "Revealed" (1:11-2:14)
    (2) The Gospel "Explained" (2:15-21)

Paul defends the accuracy of his message:
    (3) The Gospel "Defended" (3:1-5:12)
    (4) The Gospel "Applied" (5:13-6:10)

Caution (6:11-17)
Benediction (6:18)

---

[1] Luther, *Galatians*, 101.
[2] Moisés Silva, "Galatians," in *Commentary on the New Testament Use of the Old Testament*, eds. G. K. Beale and D. A. Carson (Grand Rapids: Baker Academic, 2007), 788.

It's important to note two details that will serve to guide our interpretation of 2:15–21. First, these verses are part of Paul's personal testimony which begins in 1:11. That is to say, Paul is still countering his opponents' charge that he has corrupted the gospel by refusing to teach what he had "allegedly" received from the other apostles—namely, that we must observe the OT law to have a right relationship with God. Second, these verses are part of Paul's fourth appeal which begins in 2:11. That is to say, he's still explaining what happened at Antioch when Peter refused to eat with Gentile believers out of fear of the Jews. Paul confronts him with a question: "If you, though a Jew, live like a Gentile and not like a Jew, how can you force the Gentiles to live like Jews?" (2:14).

Paul answers his own question in 2:15–21. He tells Peter that he can't force the Gentiles to live like Jews. He gives four reasons why. (1) To do so is to act contrary to what he knows (2:15–16). (2) To do so is to rebuild what has been torn down (2:17–18). (3) To do so is to deny the significance of the cross (2:19–20). (4) To do so is to imply that Christ died for no purpose (2:21).

Paul begins the entire section as follows: "We ourselves are Jews by birth and not Gentile sinners" (2:15). He's reminding Peter that the two of them belong to the OT covenant community. "Yet we know" (2:16). What do they know? (1) A person isn't justified by "works of the law" (2) A person is justified "through faith in Jesus Christ." To appreciate Paul's point, we need to answer three questions.

First, what does it mean to be "justified"? Paul uses the term three times in these verses.[3] Simply put, justification is the opposite of condemnation (Rom. 8:1, 33–34). To condemn is to declare guilty; therefore, to justify is to declare not guilty. When God justifies sinners, he puts them into a right relationship with himself. Paul affirms that God's verdict of "not guilty" on the Day of Judgment is announced in advance for those who believe in Christ.[4]

Second, what are "the works of the law"? Paul uses the expression three times in these verses.[5] Some scholars argue that "the works of the law" refer to those laws which separate Jews and Gentiles.[6] In other words, they're

---

[3] Also see 3:8, 11, 24; 5:4.

[4] For more on this, see Richard B. Gaffin Jr., *By Faith, Not By Sight: Paul and the Order of Salvation* (Wanesboro: Paternoster, 2006), 79–108.

[5] Also see 3:2, 5, 10.

[6] This is known as the New Perspective. For proponents of this view, see James Dunn, *The Theology of Paul the Apostle* (Grand Rapids: Eerdmans, 1998); Don Garlington, *An Exposition of*

strictly identity markers such as circumcision. The root problem, therefore, that plagues the churches of Galatia is ethno-centrism. While this is certainly an issue, it isn't what lies at the heart of the matter. Those who restrict "the works of the law" to specific regulations that separate Jews and Gentiles are working with a far too narrow definition. When Paul speaks of "the works of the law," he's thinking of the law in its entirety (3:10-11). The Jews are convinced that their observance of the law (i.e., human achievement) is essential for salvation. This means their religion is legalistic in essence.

Third, what is "faith in Christ"? Paul uses the expression three times in these verses.[7] In short, it's God's gift whereby we know Christ and apply Christ. We believe he is really ours. Such faith justifies because it's the instrument whereby we apprehend Christ.

With all that said, we can summarize Paul's rebuke of Peter as follows: "If you and I (members of the OT covenant community) are required to put our faith in Christ, to have a right relationship with God, then it makes no sense for you to require Gentile believers to observe the law to obtain a right relationship with God. When you withdraw from eating with Gentile believers, you're acting contrary to what you know."

Based on these verses, I want to affirm five important truths, which should serve to crystalize the doctrine of justification in our minds.

We must obey God's law
Whether we realize it or not, God placed a debt on us at creation—we owe perfect obedience to him. According to what Paul says in Romans 2:12-15, the Jews possess God's law written on stones (special revelation), while the Gentiles possess God's law written on their hearts (natural revelation). It makes no difference, in other words. Everyone possesses God's law, everyone is under obligation to obey it, and failure to do so results in condemnation. This is the necessary starting point for understanding the doctrine of justification. Again, in simple terms, we owe a debt of perfect obedience to God.

Galatians: A Reading from the New Perspective (Eugene: Wipf & Stock, 2007); and N.T. Wright, *The New Testament and the People of God* (Minneapolis: Fortress, 1992).

[7] Also see 3:2, 5, 7, 8, 9, 11, 12, 14, 22, 23, 25.

We can't obey God's law

In 2:16, Paul quotes Psalm 143:2, "Enter not into judgment with your servant, for no one living is righteous before you." Here David pleads for mercy because he realizes he can't stand before God based on his own effort. No one can. Elsewhere, Paul declares, "Those who are in the flesh cannot please God" (Rom. 8:8). Our sin (self-love) alienates us from God. It enslaves us, darkening our minds, hardening our hearts, and binding our wills. This condition is called "the flesh." It's at war with God; it's unable to obey God; and it's unable to please God. "None is righteous, no, not one" (Rom. 3:10).

We must obey God's law in the person of a mediator

Because of our inability to obey God's law, we stand in need of someone to do what we can't do. We need someone to keep God's law on our behalf. This "someone" is Christ. When John objects to Christ's request for baptism, Christ responds, "Let it be so now, for thus it is fitting for us to fulfill all righteousness" (Matt. 3:15). He doesn't need to be baptized by John, so why does he insist on it? He's about to embark on his public ministry—the salvation of his people. At the outset, he must identify with them in their sin. He was indeed "born under the law, so that he might redeem those who were under the law" (4:4–5). From his birth to his death, Christ lived "under the law," obeying every command, meeting every requirement, and fulfilling every detail. Having done so, he paid the penalty we had incurred for breaking it. This is the mediator we need.

We become one with the mediator through faith

Faith is the instrument by which we embrace Christ. It consists of two components. The first is the knowledge of Christ and his benefits. "And this is eternal life, that they know you, the only true God, and Jesus Christ whom you have sent" (John 17:3). The second is the application of Christ and his benefits. We must personally receive that which God offers us (John 1:12; 6:35). He offers Christ and all his benefits to us in the Word and sacraments (or ordinances). And, therefore, we must believe it, that is, apply it to ourselves. Believing in Christ isn't a mere decision to believe a series of propositional statements. Rather, it's coming to him, as to a spring in the desert, and drinking our fill.

God accepts the mediator's obedience as if it were ours

We owe a double debt to God: (1) we must obey his law; and (2) we must pay the penalty for having broken his law. We can't pay either debt, but our mediator has paid both on our behalf. Because we're one with Christ, God treats us as if we were Christ. Our sins are no longer ours; they're Christ's. Christ's righteousness now belongs not only to him; it belongs to us.[8] John Bunyan provides a stirring account of how this truth came alive to him:

> One day, as I was walking in the field ... with some dashes on my conscience, fearing that all was not right, suddenly this sentence fell upon my soul, "Your righteousness is in heaven." And I saw, with the eyes of my soul, Jesus Christ at God's right hand. There, I say, is my righteousness. Wherever I am, or whatever I am doing, God cannot say of me, "He lacks righteousness," for my righteousness stands before him. I also saw that it was not my good frame of heart that made my righteousness better, nor yet my bad frame of heart that made my righteousness worse; for my righteousness is Jesus Christ himself, the same yesterday, and today, and forever.[9]

This is a heart-warming truth. "O sweet exchange! O unsearchable operation! O benefits surpassing all expectation! That the wickedness of many should be hid in a single righteous One, and that the righteousness of One should justify many transgressors!"[10]

Conclusion

In Psalm 15:1, David asks, "O LORD, who shall sojourn in your tent? Who shall dwell on your holy hill?" He asks the same question in Psalm 24:3, "Who shall ascend the hill of the LORD? And who shall stand in his holy place?" The terms "tent" and "hill" (or "place") have a reference point. As David walks in the city of Jerusalem, he's conscious of a tent on a nearby hill. It's rarely out of sight, and it's never far from his mind. He erected this tent to house the Ark of the Covenant (2 Sam. 6; 1 Chron. 16). He has it in

---

[8] N.T. Wright openly rejects the "classical" doctrine of the imputation of Christ's righteousness to sinners in *What Saint Paul Really Said: Was Saul of Tarsus the Real Founder of Christianity?* (Grand Rapids: Eerdmans, 1997). For a reply, see John Piper, *The Future of Justification: A Response to N.T. Wright* (Wheaton: Crossway Books, 2007).

[9] John Bunyan, *Grace Abounding to the Chief of Sinners* (Middlesex: Echo Library, 2006), 57.

[10] *The Epistle of Mathetes to Diognetus*, in *Ante-Nicene Fathers*, eds. Alexander Roberts & James Donaldson, 10 vols (Peabody: Hendrickson, 2004), 1:28.

view when he asks: "O LORD, who shall sojourn in your tent? Who shall dwell on your holy hill?"

While the Israelites were gathered at the base of Sinai, God gave Moses detailed instructions concerning the construction of the tabernacle. It consists of a three-fold division. (1) The outer court is where the altar and the laver stand. (2) The Holy Place contains the candlestick, the table of showbread, and the altar of incense. (3) The Most Holy Place contains the Ark of the Covenant. This is where God manifests his glory in a cloud.

This three-fold division mirrors Israel's experience at Sinai. (1) The people gather around the base of Sinai, corresponding to the outer court. (2) The elders ascend to the mid-way point of Sinai, corresponding to the priests' access to the Holy Place. (3) Moses ascends to the summit of Sinai, corresponding to the high priest's access to the Most Holy Place. He alone enters the Most Holy Place once a year on the Day of Atonement.

The tabernacle, therefore, is designed to remind the Israelites of Sinai. Moses alone ascends to God at the summit. Similarly, the high priest alone ascends to God in the Most Holy Place. No one else is permitted to enter God's presence. That's why David asks, "O LORD, who shall sojourn in your tent? Who shall dwell on your holy hill?" He's conscious of his unworthiness due to his sin. He knows that only a righteous man can enter God's presence.

David's question anticipates Christ's coming into the world. He alone can "sojourn" in God's tent. He alone can "dwell" on God's holy hill. He alone can enter God's presence because he alone is righteous. Mercifully, he offered himself upon Calvary's cross to make atonement for those who have broken God's law, for those who are unrighteous, for those who have no right to enter God's presence, for those who have no claim to God's mercy. God now offers Christ to sinners. He makes this offer audibly in the Word and visibly in the sacraments. "Whoever calls on the name of the Lord shall be saved" (Rom. 10:13). We aren't required to fulfill any conditions, nor are we required to produce our own righteousness. We're commanded to receive Christ through faith. Upon doing so, we're implanted into him. We take possession of all the benefits and blessings that are found in him. Chief among these is the wonderful reality that we become the righteousness of God in Christ (2 Cor. 5:21). Now we declare with David: "Blessed is the one whose transgression is forgiven, whose sin is covered. Blessed is the man against whom the LORD counts no iniquity" (Ps. 32:1-2; Rom. 4:7-8). And now we sing:

Justified in Christ (2:15–21)

Mine by covenant, mine forever,
Mine by oath, and mine by blood,
Mine—nor time the bond shall sever,
Mine as an unchanging God.
My Redeemer!
O how sweet to call thee mine![11]

---

[11] Henry Thomas Smart, "My Redeemer" (hymn).

6
Crucified with Christ (2:15-21)

In the words of J.I. Packer, "The taproot of our entire salvation is our union with Christ by the Holy Spirit."[1] This means our salvation is *positional*. We've been implanted into Christ. His dying and rising are ours, that is, God imputes them to us as if we had performed them in our own persons. It also means our salvation is *transformational*. We've been implanted into Christ. The indwelling Holy Spirit now empowers us to express new desires in action, namely, Christ-like character. It's crucial to keep this two-fold emphasis in mind as we return to 2:15-21.

While visiting the city of Antioch, Peter refuses to eat with Gentile believers out of fear of offending certain Jews. His actions might seem harmless, but they're serious because they imply that it's necessary to observe the OT law to have a right standing with God. Paul dismantles any such notion in 2:15-21. He speaks directly to Peter and indirectly to his opponents and to the churches of Galatia. Essentially, he levies four charges against Peter.

You're acting contrary to what you know (2:15-16). "Peter, you and I know two things. First, we know that a person isn't justified by the works of the law. Second, we know that a person is justified through faith in Christ. If Jews (like you and me) need to put their faith in Christ to have a right relationship with God, then obviously Gentiles need to do the same. Yet, your actions (i.e., refusing to eat with Gentiles) imply that they need to observe the law to have a right relationship with God. Peter, you're acting contrary to what you know."

You're rebuilding what you already tore down (2:17-18). "Peter, you and I know that the law reveals our sin and demonstrates our need to be justified in Christ. This doesn't make Christ a promoter of sin. On the contrary, those who attempt to rebuild the law (now that Christ has come) are the ones who openly violate God's will. They deny the fact that righteousness is found in

---

[1] J.I. Packer, "The Atonement in the Christian Life," in *In My Place Condemned He Stood: Celebrating the Glory of the Atonement*, eds. Mark Dever and J.I. Packer (Wheaton: Crossway, 2008), 417.

Christ alone. That's what you're doing by refusing to eat with Gentiles. You're forcing them to live under the law. Peter, you're rebuilding what you already tore down."

You're denying the significance of the cross (2:19–20). "Peter, you and I know that the reign of law ends through the law. This is the case because Christ takes the penalty of the law upon himself and pays it. In so doing, he ends the era of the law. Those who believe in Christ share in this victory because they're united to him. You and I are dead to the law, meaning we're no longer under its dominion and condemnation. Do you not see the implications of your actions? Peter, you're denying the significance of the cross."

You're saying that Christ died for no purpose (2:21). "Peter, you and I know that the law is dead to us because our identity is now found in the crucified Saviour. But you deny this by your actions. You give the impression that it's necessary to keep the law to obtain a right standing with God. If that's the case, the obvious implication is that Christ's death is unnecessary for justification. Peter, you're saying that Christ died for no purpose."

That's a simple overview of Paul's account of how he confronted Peter at Antioch. Of note, it includes one of the most succinct descriptions of the Christian life in all of Scripture: "I have been crucified with Christ. It is no longer I who live, but Christ who lives in me. And the life I now live in the flesh I live by faith in the Son of God, who loved me and gave himself for me" (2:20). I encourage you to notice five facts.

"I have been crucified with Christ"

Paul wasn't physically present at Calvary's cross, so what does he mean? "Do you not know that all of us who have been baptized into Christ Jesus were baptized into his death?" (Rom. 6:3). His point is that we were baptized into Christ when we believed in him. The implication is that we're now one with Christ in God's sight. Because of this union, Christ's death is our death, meaning it's reckoned to be ours. That's why Paul can say, "I have been crucified with Christ." His use of the perfect tense is significant, as it points to the abiding influence of the cross in the believer's life. Upon the cross, Christ stood in our place. Because of our union with him through faith, his cross is made ours. It's as though we have been crucified in our own person.[2]

---

[2] See Matthew 10:38; Luke 9:23; Romans 6:6; 1 Corinthians 1:17–18; 2 Corinthians 13:4; Philippians 3:18; Hebrews 12:1–2; 13:3.

"It is no longer I who live"

This doesn't mean that Paul lost his personality, but that he no longer identified with Adam (the old man) because he identified with Christ (the new man). As a result, he no longer lives for himself. "We were buried therefore with him by baptism into death, in order that, just as Christ was raised from the dead by the glory of the Father, we too might walk in newness of life" (Rom. 6:4). Our old life in Adam is now dead. It's a "legal" death—something that happened by virtue of our union with Christ. We're baptized into his death, meaning the merit of his death is ours, and the penalty of our sin is paid in full.

"But Christ who lives in me"

Because we're crucified legally with Christ, our "body of sin" is done away with (Rom. 6:6). The result is we're no longer "slaves to sin." As Paul says, "One who has died has been set free from sin" (Rom. 6:7). In other words, sin is no longer the governing principle within us. Christ lived under submission to the Holy Spirit. Now he sends the Holy Spirit to help us to do the same, meaning we live out our new identity in Christ by the power of the Holy Spirit (5:16–24). Peter Toon provides a helpful explanation of what this entails:

> Christ was filled and constantly re-filled with the Holy Spirit. The Holy Spirit was the source in him not only of ministerial gifts but also of meekness and lowliness of heart/mind. The Holy Spirit continues to fill his human nature as he lives in heaven. Raised from the dead by the Spirit of holiness (Rom. 1:4) and exalted into heaven in his glorified human body/nature, Jesus is still filled (and as man is continually being filled) with the Holy Spirit. Thus, he remains the One—the Holy One—from and through whom the Holy Spirit goes forth to act in and upon those who believe the good news of salvation. God the Father sends the Holy Spirit via the Lord Jesus to the world: so the Spirit descends and works among human beings as the Spirit of Christ, bearing his name and distributing his power, virtues, and characteristics.[3]

"And the life I now live in the flesh I live by faith of the Son of God"

Although we're united to Christ (and belong to the age to come), we still live in "the present evil age" (1:4). The spiritual life, therefore, is one of tension.

---

[3] Peter Toon, *What is Spirituality? And is it for me?* (London: Daybreak, 1989), 58-59.

We're called to live by faith, submitting to Christ who dwells in us by the Holy Spirit. As Graeme Goldsworthy observes, "Christ ... becomes our other identity, our *alter ego*. We possess and know this other self only by faith."[4]

"Who loved me and gave himself for me"

The focus of our faith is Christ's love (1:3–5), which serves as the necessary motivation for the life of faith. "By this we know love, that he laid down his life for us" (1 John 3:16). According to Jonathan Edwards, "There are two things that make Christ's love so wonderful: (1) that he should be willing to endure suffering that was so great; and (2) that he should be willing to endure it to make atonement for wickedness that was so great."[5] It is this "sacrificial love" that "serves as fuel for [our] faith-filled obedience."[6]

Conclusion

Based on what Paul says in 2:20, we discover that the key to the Christian life is simply this: (1) believing that Christ was crucified for us; (2) believing that we've been crucified with Christ; (3) seeing ourselves hanging on the cross; and (4) living accordingly. The implications are numerous.

First, we're to behave as dead men in respect to our sin. "I have been crucified with Christ." In effect, God says to us: "Because you believe, I have united you to Christ by the Holy Spirit. When he died, you died. When he rose, you rose. Now, act like it!" What does this mean for our struggle with sin? What does it mean for envy, anger, and bitterness? What does it mean for lust, greed, and impatience? What does it mean for unguarded words and unfiltered thoughts? Do we see ourselves hanging on the cross? Do we see all that we were in Adam breathing its last breath?

Second, we're to behave as dead men in respect to our will. "I have been crucified with Christ." Therefore, we live to do God's will, and we exchange our will for his will. Many of us think we'll be miserable if we deny ourselves, but the Bible makes it clear that blessedness lies in self-giving. How does this apply in our home, church, and workplace? How does it apply to how we use our money, time, gifts, talents, and abilities?

---

[4] Graeme Goldsworthy, *According to Plan: The Unfolding Revelation of God in the Bible* (Downers Grove: Inter-Varsity Press, 1991), 221.

[5] Jonathan Edwards, *The Works of Jonathan Edwards*, 2 vols (1834; rpt., Peabody: Hendrickson, 1998), 2:870.

[6] Paul McClendon, *Paul's Spirituality in Galatians* (Eugene: Wipf & Stock, 2015), 123.

CRUCIFIED WITH CHRIST (2:15-21)

Third, we're to behave as dead men in respect to the world. "I have been crucified with Christ." The present age (the world) is characterized by a system of perspectives, expectations, convictions, and actions, which make man the focus while relegating God to the periphery. We aren't to be conformed to this world but be transformed by the renewing of our minds (Rom. 12:2). We set our minds on Christ—all we are and will be in him. We think in an entirely new way. Who am I? What am I doing? What do I want? What do I value? When we come to Christ, he reorients our values, dreams, priorities, and opinions.

Fourth, we're to behave as dead men in respect to offenses. "I have been crucified with Christ." How do we react when people disagree with us or mistreat us? What about when people are selfish, unfair, abrupt, or insensitive? Do we take offense? Do we seek revenge? Do we become snarky and sarcastic? Do we insist on our own way? Do we insist on our rights? "Do nothing from selfish ambition or conceit, but in humility count others more significant than yourselves. Let each of you look not only to his own interests, but also to the interests of others" (Phil. 2:3-4). The power of Christ crucified shapes all our relationships.

Fifth, we're to behave as dead men in respect to comforts. "I have been crucified with Christ." The world tells us that our purpose is to play, collect stuff, and pursue a life of ease and comfort. Many of us think to ourselves: "I don't want opposition; I want approval. I don't want shame; I want honour. I don't want suffering; I want comfort and pleasure in this world right now. And I don't want to die; I want to be safe, to be secure, and to stay alive."[7] We're bombarded with a very simple message in our day: personal gratification will make us happy. But Christ says the opposite: personal sacrifice (not gratification) is the key to happiness (Luke 9:23).

Sixth, we're to behave as dead men in respect to afflictions. "I have been crucified with Christ." We share in his suffering, and we become like him in his suffering. He suffered in faith—that is, in dependence on his Father's goodness. He suffered humbly, willingly, and lovingly. Why? He had God's glory in view. Suffering isn't just the way Christ triumphs; it's the way we triumph. By placing our hope in him, we persevere through life's manifold challenges.

---

[7] https://www.desiringgod.org/messages/sacred-schizophrenia.

This is the transformational effect of the gospel—we follow a crucified Saviour by living a crucified life. "I have been crucified with Christ. It is no longer I who live, but Christ who lives in me. And the life I now live in the flesh I live by faith in the Son of God, who loved me and gave himself for me" (2:20).

Section 3:
The Gospel "Defended" (3:1–5:12)

7
The Gift of the Holy Spirit (3:1–5)

We've been following a very simple outline in our study of Paul's Epistle to the Galatians:

Salutation (1:1–5)
Caution (1:6–10)

Paul defends the authority of his mission:
    (1) The Gospel "Revealed" (1:11–2:14)
    (2) The Gospel "Explained" (2:15–21)

Paul defends the accuracy of his message:
    (3) The Gospel "Defended" (3:1–5:12)
    (4) The Gospel "Applied" (5:13–6:10)

Caution (6:11–17)
Benediction (6:18)

We've completed our study of the Gospel Revealed (1:11–2:14) and the Gospel Explained (2:15–21). In this chapter, we arrive at the Gospel Defended (3:1–5:12). Paul begins, "O foolish Galatians! Who has bewitched you?" (3:1). The term "bewitched" isn't found anywhere else in the NT. It literally means "to cast a spell over someone, or to hold someone spellbound by an irresistible power." The Galatians are bewitched, meaning they're no longer able to see the obvious. Their vision is clouded, and their perception is stunted. The issue isn't a lack of information, but a lack of discernment.

What is the *cause* of their bewitchment? Paul doesn't state it here, but he does elsewhere. "I am afraid that as the serpent deceived Eve by his cunning, your thoughts will be led astray from a sincere and pure devotion to Christ" (2 Cor. 11:3). All disorder is ultimately the devil's handiwork.

What is the *cure* for their bewitchment? It calls for *tough* love. "O foolish Galatians! Who has bewitched you?" Or, as J.B. Phillips translates it: "O you dear idiots of Galatia … surely you cannot be so idiotic?" Paul attempts to stir them from their bewitchment by presenting four main arguments, followed by an appeal.

An Argument from Experience (3:1–5)
"Did you receive the Spirit by works of the law or by hearing with faith?" (3:3)

An Argument from Scripture (3:6–4:7)
"Is the law then contrary to the promise of God?" (3:21)

An Argument from Experience (4:8–20)
"What then has become of the blessing you felt?" (4:15)

An Argument from Scripture (4:21–31)
"Do you not listen to the law?" (4:21)

An Appeal (5:1–12)

Paul begins his first argument by reminding the Galatians that "it was before [their] eyes that Jesus Christ was publicly portrayed as crucified" (3:1). For Paul, the phrases "Christ crucified" and "the cross of Christ" represent the whole doctrine of the gospel.[1] He is, therefore, reminding them that he had proclaimed among them that Christ's life and death are the only procuring cause of salvation for all who believe. But what has happened since his departure? They've drifted away from the sole sufficiency of Christ for salvation.

To show them their folly, Paul asks four rhetorical questions. (1) "Did you receive the Spirit by works of the law or by hearing with faith?" (3:2). *Assumed Answer:* "We received the Spirit by hearing with faith." (2) "Having begun by the Spirit, are you now being perfected by the flesh?" (3:3). *Assumed Answer:* "No, we aren't being perfected by the flesh. That would be a foolish endeavour, seeing as the flesh contributes nothing to salvation." (3) "Did you suffer so many things in vain—if indeed it was in vain?" (3:4). *Assumed Answer:* "No, we didn't suffer in vain. It would be absurd to reject the very thing for which we've suffered so much." (4) "Does he who supplies the Spirit to you and works miracles among you do so by the works of the law, or by hearing with faith?" (3:5). *Assumed Answer:* "He does so by hearing with faith."

---

[1] See 1 Corinthians 1:23; 2:2.

The Gift of the Holy Spirit (3:1-5)

All told, Paul shows them the unreasonableness of deserting faith in Christ (by which they received the Holy Spirit) and returning to the works of the law (by which they never received the Holy Spirit). Their own experience confirms the truth of the gospel. But now, they're turning from the substance to the shadow and from the mature to the immature. As John Brown explains, "For the Jew to become a Christian was for the child to become a man—a natural, desirable course. For the Christian to become a Jew is for the man voluntarily to sink into a second childhood—a most unnatural and undesirable course."[2]

When we lose sight of Christ as the sole grounds of our justification and faith as the sole means of our justification, we quickly fall into the same error as the Galatians. To avoid this pitfall, we need to keep three questions before us.

Have we seen Christ publicly portrayed as crucified (3:1)?

Christ "gave himself for our sins to deliver us from the present evil age, according to the will of our God and Father" (1:4). We hear it whenever God's Word is preached, and we see it whenever the Lord's Supper is celebrated. Is it vivid? When Christ is publicly portrayed as crucified, three things happen.

It produces conviction

When we see Christ publicly portrayed as crucified, we see God's wrath. "He condemned sin in the flesh"—that is, in Christ who came "in the likeness of sinful flesh" (Rom. 8:3). There's a profound truth in Rembrandt's painting, *The Raising of the Cross*. It depicts the Roman soldiers hoisting the cross into place. In the background stands a priest, encircled by the mocking crowds and grieving women. At Christ's feet stands an out-of-place man wearing a blue painter's hat. He's helping the soldiers set the cross in place. It's Rembrandt. He painted himself into the scene as one of those who crucified Christ. He was declaring a profound truth: Christ was "bruised for our iniquities" (Isa. 53:5).

> He took my sins and my sorrows.
> He made them his very own;
> He bore the burden to Calvary.

---

[2] John Brown, *An Exposition of the Epistle to the Galatians* (Evansville: The Sovereign Grace Book Club, 1957), 111.

The Fullness of Time

And suffered and died alone.[3]

It produces comfort

When we see Christ publicly portrayed as crucified, we see God's love. "In this is love, not that we have loved God but that he loved us and sent his Son to be the propitiation for our sins" (1 John 4:10). Because of his love, he left a glorious crown and walked in our flesh. Because of his love, he was hungry, thirsty, and weary. Because of his love, he was sorrowful unto death. Because of his love, he was betrayed, arrested, and condemned. Because of his love, he was crowned with thorns, scourged with whips, and pierced with nails. Because of his love, he hung on a shameful cross, bearing our guilt. Because of his love, he "poured out his soul to death" (Isa. 53:12).

Christ's crucifixion is the public display of God's love for us. "He is our most loving Father," writes John Owen. "Every other discovery of God, without this, will but make the soul flee from him; but if the heart is much taken up with the eminency of the Father's love, it cannot choose but be overpowered, conquered, and endeared unto him ... Exercise your thoughts upon this very thing, the eternal, free, and fruitful love of the Father, and see if your heart is not wrought upon to delight in him."[4]

It produces change

When we see Christ publicly portrayed as crucified, we're compelled to change. "Christ took our misery that we might have his glory."[5] This realization compels us to love him, and out of love to obey him. Elsewhere, Paul declares that nothing can separate us from God's love in Christ (Rom. 8:31-39). Separation means division (or divorce). But Christ never divorces his bride. It is an eternal union, based upon an eternal love. We can rest assured that his love for us doesn't depend on anything in us. As a matter of fact, we spoil his love when we think it's induced by anything in us. R.C. Sproul explains, "God does not love us because we are lovely. He loves us because Christ is lovely. He loves us in Christ."[6] He loves us because we're one with his Beloved. As the Holy Spirit impresses this wonderful truth upon us, our

---

[3] Charles Hutchinson Gabriel, "I Stand Amazed in the Presence" (hymn).
[4] John Owen, *Communion with the Triune God*, eds. Kelly Kapic and Justin Taylor (1657; Wheaton: Crossway, 2007), 127-128.
[5] Thomas Manton, *The Works of Thomas Manton*, 22 vols (Birmingham: Solid Ground Christian Books, 2008), 3:266.
[6] R.C. Sproul, *Loved by God* (Nashville: Word Publishing, 2001), 35.

The Gift of the Holy Spirit (3:1-5)

love for God grows, and correspondingly, our desire to know and obey his will.

Have we received the Holy Spirit by hearing with faith (3:2)?

According to Thomas Schreiner, "The reception of the Holy Spirit, as Paul argues in this paragraph, functions as the decisive evidence that the Galatians are justified by faith."[7] They received the Holy Spirit by "hearing with faith." Faith, therefore, is the instrument through which they were brought into vital union with Christ and received the promised blessing.

Paul declares, "For in [*en*] one Spirit we were all baptized into [*eis*] one body—Jews or Greeks, slaves or free—and all were made to drink into one Spirit" (1 Cor. 12:13). Here Paul uses two prepositions. The first is *en*, which means "in" or "with." It indicates the *element* in which the baptism occurs. The second is *eis*, which means "into" or "towards." It indicates the *purpose* for which the baptism occurs. In sum, Christ is the *agent* by which the baptism occurs, the Holy Spirit is the *element* in which the baptism occurs, and identity in "one body" (i.e., the church) is the *purpose* for which the baptism occurs.

This baptism is a once for all experience that occurs when we come to Christ.[8] John the Baptist refers to Christ as "he who baptizes with the Holy Spirit" (John 1:33). He again uses a present participle when describing Christ as "the Lamb of God, who takes away the sin of the world" (John 1:29). These statements provide a description of Christ's twofold ministry: "a taking away of sin and a baptizing with the Holy Spirit."[9] Peter proclaims these same two blessings: "Repent and be baptized every one of you in the name of Jesus Christ for the forgiveness of your sins, and you will receive the gift of the Holy Spirit" (Acts 2:38).[10]

Are we being perfected by the flesh or the Spirit (3:3)?

Both justification and sanctification are the result of union with Christ. The Holy Spirit sanctifies us by illumining our darkened mind, liberating our enslaved will, and directing our disordered affections. This renewal doesn't make us perfect. While it's true that sanctification breaks sin's dominion

---

[7] Schreiner, *Galatians*, 177.
[8] See Romans 8:9, 11; 1 Corinthians 6:19; Galatians 3:2; 4:6; 2 Timothy 1:14.
[9] John R. W. Stott, *Baptism and Fullness* (London: Inter-Varsity, 1975), 24.
[10] See Ezekiel 36:25-27.

over us, it doesn't eradicate sin in us. Future glorification alone will mark the termination of our sin. At present, we're engaged in a great conflict between the "flesh" (love of self) and the "Spirit" (love of God).

"For if you live according to the flesh you will die," writes Paul, "but if by the Spirit you put to death the deeds of the body, you will live" (Rom. 8:13). The verb "putting to death" is in the present tense, meaning sanctification is a continuous battle with sin. We can only engage in this battle with the help of the Holy Spirit who works in us and with us. John Owen counsels:

> All other ways of mortification are vain, all helps leave us helpless; it must be done by the Spirit. Men, as the apostle intimates (Rom. 9:30-32), may attempt this work on other principles, by means and advantages administered on other accounts, as they always have done, and do: but, saith he, "This is the work of the Spirit; by him alone is it to be wrought, and by no other power is it to be brought about."[11]

How does the Holy Spirit enable us to mortify sin? He does so by fanning the flames of our love for God to such a degree that sin becomes the object of our hate; that is to say, he heightens our love for God by revealing his "excellencies" to us. "Be confident of this," writes George Swinnock, "the more you know of the excellencies of God, the more you will prize his Son, submit to his Spirit, crucify the flesh, condemn the world, fear to offend him, study to please him, the more holy you will be in all manner of conversation."[12]

Conclusion

Have we been bewitched by a legalistic view of salvation? Paul makes it clear that we're justified by grace alone (the cause) through faith alone (the means) in Christ alone (the grounds). And it is "by hearing with faith" that we've received the promised Holy Spirit.

> I sighed for rest and happiness,
> I yearned for them, not thee;
> But while I passed my Saviour by,
> His love laid hold of me.

---

[11] John Owen, *The Works of John Owen*, ed. W. H. Gould, 16 vols (London, 1850; rpt., Edinburgh: Banner of Truth, 1977), 6:7.

[12] George Swinnock, *The Works of George Swinnock*, ed. James Nichol, 5 vols (London, 1868; rpt., Edinburgh: Banner of Truth, 1992), 3:156.

The Gift of the Holy Spirit (3:1-5)

I tried the broken cisterns, Lord,
But, ah, the waters failed!
Even as I stopped to drink, they fled,
And mocked me as I wailed.

Now none but Christ can satisfy,
None other name for me!
There's love and life and lasting joy,
Lord Jesus, found in thee.[13]

---

[13] Emma Bevan, "O Christ in Thee My Soul Hath Found" (hymn).

8
The Blessing of Abraham (3:6–14)

According to Martin Luther,

> Trying to be justified by the law is like counting money out of an empty purse, eating and drinking from an empty dish and cup, looking for strength and riches where there is nothing but weakness and poverty, laying a burden on someone who is already oppressed to the point of collapse, trying to spend a hundred gold pieces and not having a pittance.[1]

Given the extent of our sin, any attempt to be justified by our own effort is an exercise in futility. "Our sinful condition," explains John Piper, "is the commitment to be our own god. ... I will be the final authority in my life. I will decide what is right and wrong for me, what is good and bad for me, and what is true and false for me. And my desires will express my sovereignty, autonomy, and (though I don't dare admit it) deity."[2] Given our sinful condition, we can't be justified by the law. We must, therefore, look to someone to do what we can't do. We must look to someone who has fulfilled God's law—Christ.

When we become one with Christ through faith, a transaction takes place. What's ours becomes his, and what's his becomes ours. Paul writes to Onesimus, asking him to welcome back Philemon: "If he has wronged you at all, or owes you anything, charge that to my account" (Philem. 1:18). Because of our union with Christ, our sin is charged to his account and his righteousness is charged to our account. This makes the sole sufficiency of Christ central to the gospel.

It was this truth that the Galatian churches were in danger of forfeiting by listening to those who insisted upon performing the works of the OT law for justification. As we observed in the last chapter, Paul demonstrates the futility of such thinking by an argument from experience (Gal. 3:1–5). He asks,

---

[1] Luther, *Galatians*, 406–407.
[2] John Piper, *The Satisfied Soul: Showing the Supremacy of God in All of Life* (New York: Multnomah, 2017), 321.

"Did you receive the Spirit by works of the law or by hearing with faith?" (3:2). The answer is obvious: "by hearing with faith" (3:5). The inference is also obvious: Why would anyone want to submit to the law?

In his second argument, Paul appeals to Scripture by turning his readers' attention to the towering OT patriarch, Abraham (3:6–4:7). His goal is to correct their thinking by clarifying what Scripture says about three important subjects. (1) What is the blessing of Abraham and who are its recipients (3:6–14)? (2) What is the precise relationship between God's promise to Abraham and the Mosaic law (3:15–26)? (3) Who are the offspring of Abraham (3:27–4:7)?

Paul clarifies the first by appealing to six OT Scriptures.[3]

Scripture 1 (3:6–7)

"Abraham believed God, and it was counted to him as righteousness" (Gen. 15:6).

The false teachers in the churches of Galatia insist that observance of the OT law (particularly circumcision) is necessary to be counted among God's people. Paul sets the record straight by going back to Abraham. How did Abraham obtain a right standing in God's sight? We learn from Genesis 15:6 that God reckoned Abraham to be a believer and, therefore, he treated Abraham as though he were righteous.

What's the obvious implication? "Know then that it is those of faith who are the sons of Abraham."

Scripture 2 (3:8–9)

"In you shall all the nations be blessed" (Gen. 12:3; 17:4; 18:18).

Abraham's faith wasn't some theoretical belief in God, but a belief in God's specific promise that a descendant (i.e., Christ) would arrive in the line of his son, Isaac, to bless all nations. He understood that God would bless the nations just as he had blessed him—namely, through faith. This is precisely what Christ told the Jews: "Your father Abraham rejoiced that he would see my day. He saw it and was glad" (John 8:56). With Christ's coming, the promise is fulfilled, and the nations receive the promised blessing by believing like Abraham.

---

[3] For an analysis of these OT texts, see the various commentaries on Paul's Epistle to the Galatians, esp. Silva, "Galatians," 791–803.

The Blessing of Abraham (3:6–14)

What's the obvious implication? "So then, those who are of faith are blessed along with Abraham, the man of faith."

Scripture 3 (3:10)
"Cursed be everyone who does not abide by all things written in the Book of the Law" (Deut. 27:26; 28:58-60).

Here Paul makes it clear that anyone who fails to observe everything written in the OT law is cursed. Since no one observes everything written in the law, everyone is cursed. That being the case, why would anyone look to the OT law as a means of salvation? It can condemn us, but it can't justify us. It can wound us, but it can't heal us.

What's the obvious implication? "All who rely on the works of the law are under a curse."

Scripture 4 (3:11)
"The righteous shall live by faith" (Hab. 2:4).

Given that no one abides by "all things written in the law," how can a anyone stand before God on the judgment day? How can anyone be assured of God's acceptance? Paul tells us that the righteous person lives by faith. In other words, a right standing with God can't be through the law because Scripture clearly teaches that it's through faith. No one has ever been justified apart from faith. We're justified through faith because it unites us to Christ who's righteous.

What's the obvious implication? "Now it is evident that no one is justified before God by the law."

Scripture 5 (3:12)
"The one who does them shall live by them" (Lev. 18:5).

Why did God command the Jews to follow the OT law if it couldn't save them? It required perfect obedience, but it also provided forgiveness through the sacrificial system. But these sacrifices pointed ahead to Christ. Since Christ has come and atoned for sin, the sacrificial system is now obsolete. Thus, those who place themselves under the law must keep the law perfectly because there's no longer any forgiveness through the sacrificial system. "The one who does them shall live by them." Paul is showing them how irrational it is for them to place themselves under the OT law. Those who do so can't perform what it requires.

What's the obvious implication? "The law is not of faith."[4]

Scripture 6 (3:13)
"Cursed is everyone who is hanged on a tree" (Deut. 21:23).

If we can't keep the law perfectly, and if the law makes no provision for forgiveness, and if we're cursed in God's sight, what are we going to do? Our predicament is hopeless. But praise God! "Cursed is everyone who is hanged on a tree." Hanging wasn't a method of execution, but what was done to a criminal after execution. It symbolized the fact that he wasn't worthy to have his feet touch the ground. Christ was "hanged on a tree" thereby symbolizing that he bore the curse on our behalf. God displayed him publicly as a propitiation in his blood (Rom. 3:25). That makes Christ our only hope for salvation.

What's the obvious implication? "Christ redeemed us from the curse of the law by becoming a curse for us."

Conclusion
Here then is the summation of Paul's entire argument: "So that in Christ Jesus the blessing of Abraham might come to the Gentiles, so that we might receive the promised Spirit through faith" (3:14). We can state it as follows. (1) God made a promise to Abraham. (2) God's promise to Abraham has become a reality in Christ. (3) The blessing of Abraham belongs to all those who believe in Christ. (4) Justification is clearly by grace alone through faith alone in Christ alone. (5) The suggestion that people must observe the OT law to enjoy a right standing with God makes no sense. (6) The Gentiles are included in the promised blessing through faith in Christ. (7) This is evident by the fact that they've received the Holy Spirit.[5]

Yet again, Christ's sole sufficiency steps to the front in Paul's defense of the gospel. A sight of our sin is indeed humbling. It can also be paralyzing. But when we look to Christ's infinite merit, our sinfulness doesn't cripple us. We know that, in Christ, God doesn't despise a broken heart. He redeems us and receives us as sons. The blessing of Abraham has come to us. "All things are yours ... the world or life or death or the present or the future—all are yours, and you are Christ's, and Christ is God's" (1 Cor. 3:21–23). Christ is

---

[4] This should not be interpreted as a wholesale repudiation of the OT law. Paul's point is simply that life doesn't come by keeping the law but believing in Christ.

[5] See Isaiah 44:3; Ezekiel 36:27; Joel 2:28.

God's—he's God's Son, God's Word, God's image, God's beloved. We're Christ's—we're his bride, his body, his brother. All things are ours because we belong to Christ who belongs to God who possesses all things. The implications are staggering.

The world is ours. God is the Creator and Governor of this world. All that exists in it is ours because Christ is the heir of all things and we're co-heirs with him. Moreover, all that happens in this world is ours, in that it serves for our eternal good (Rom. 8:28).

Life is ours. God is the author and sustainer of all life. Every moment, every day, every year, every event, every experience, is in his hands. These things aren't purposeless, meaningless, or rudderless. God uses all of life to reveal his glory in us and to us.

Death is ours. God determines the number of our days. He determines "when" and "how" we die. But the sting of death has been removed in Christ. It no longer terrifies us, controls us, or masters us. Rather, it serves us by ushering us into Christ's presence.

The present is ours. God governs all things according to the counsel of his will (Eph. 1:11). This includes all that happens in life—our sad and happy moments, our unpleasant and pleasant moments, our lonely and celebratory moments, etc. We aren't slaves of time or circumstance. All things serve one ultimate end—to make us glorious in Christ.

The future is ours. God is beyond all time and space, and dwells in one indivisible moment called eternity. He knows nothing of before or after. The future is in his hands. We'll inherit a new heaven and a new earth. We'll have bodies like Christ's glorious body. There will be no sound of weeping and no cry of distress. There will be no tension, division, turmoil, conflict, or death. God will be the everlasting light—the earth will be filled with the knowledge of his glory.

All of this is ours because we belong to Christ who belongs to God. All of this is ours because we're one with Christ who is the promised seed of Abraham.

9
The Priority of Abraham (3:15–26)

When I visit the dentist, I can't relax until I hear her say, "Everything looks good." Those words are like music to my ears. A while back, she poked around before quickly announcing, "Everything looks good." I exhaled. But her assessment and my excitement were premature. Upon checking the x-ray, she informed me that there was a problem with one tooth. The x-ray provided a fuller, clearer, and deeper picture.

Where am I going with this? The law functions like an x-ray. Each of us has formulated in our minds what we perceive to be an acceptable standard of behaviour. Convincing ourselves that we meet this standard, we conclude, "Everything looks good." But God's law functions like an x-ray, in that it shows us what we really are. It penetrates beyond our standards to our secrets. It penetrates beyond our external conduct to our internal thoughts, desires, and motives. And it reveals that we have a problem.

When the dentist informs me that there's a problem, I have a choice. I can let her fix it, or I can live in denial. It's the same way with the law. It shows us that there's a problem. We can look for help, or we can live in denial. God's law shows us our sinfulness, so that we might recognize our guilt, despair of saving ourselves, and seek a Saviour. Martin Luther declares,

> God must have a mighty hammer to crush the rocks ... that is, to crush that stubborn and perverse beast, presumption. When a man has been brought to nothing by this pounding, despairs of his own powers, righteousness, and works, and trembles before God, he will, in his terror, begin to thirst for mercy and forgiveness of sins.[1]

This "mighty hammer" is the law. What does it say? Quite simply, it tells us that we must love God with all our heart, soul, mind, and strength, and that we must love our neighbour as ourselves (Matt. 22:37-38). And it tells us that we don't love like this. It tells us that there's none righteous, no not

---

[1] Luther, *Galatians*, 310.

one, and it tells us that there's none who does good, no not one (Rom. 3:10-18). It tells us all this to crush us—especially, our presumption. What's the result? We become poor-in-spirit; we become aware of our sinfulness in the light of God's holiness; we begin to mourn on account of our sin; we become meek, meaning we recognize that anything short of eternal damnation is a mercy; and we begin to hunger and thirst after righteousness (Matt. 5:3-6). And we discover that this longing is satisfied by Christ alone.

> Now none but Christ can satisfy,
> None other name for me;
> There's love and life and lasting joy,
> Lord Jesus, found in thee.[2]

There are false teachers in the churches of Galatia who deny this. Their denial is explained in part by their misunderstanding of the function of the OT law. They think God gave it to show us that we receive the promised inheritance based on human effort. In our text, Paul sets them straight by prioritizing God's promise to Abraham.[3] He makes three key-points.

The law doesn't supersede the promise (3:15-18)

First, Paul tells them that the OT law doesn't alter God's promise to Abraham. To explain this, he appeals to a "human example," namely, the fact that once a covenant is ratified, no one "annuls it or adds to it" (3:15). God justified Abraham on account of his faith, and God promised that he would do the same for all the nations. That covenant has been ratified. The law in no way changes it. There are two important implications.

First, the promise (not the law) takes precedence (3:15, 17). God gave the promise to Abraham, Isaac, and Jacob. He gave the law to Moses, 430 years later. Therefore, the law doesn't replace or supersede the promise.

Second, the promise (not the law) guarantees the inheritance (3:16, 18).[4] God gave the promise to Christ and all who are one with him through faith (1 Cor. 1:20; Eph. 1:3). God's intent in giving the law wasn't to alter, change, or

---

[2] Emma Frances Shuttleworth Bevan, "O Christ, In Thee My Soul hath Found" (hymn).
[3] See Genesis 3:15; 12:2; 13:16; 15:5; 17:7; 22:17-18; 26:4-5; 28:14.
[4] Does the promise refer ultimately to Canaan or the whole world? See Psalm 22:27-28; 47:7-9; 72:8-11; Zephaniah. 3:9-10. See the various commentaries on Paul's Epistle to the Galatians for further discussion.

modify this promise. As a matter of fact, it's by means of the promise alone that the promised inheritance comes.

The law doesn't modify the promise (3:19–20)
Second, Paul tells them where the law fits in God's plan. "Why then the law?" The answer: "It was added because of transgressions" (3:19).[5] What does this mean? John Brown provides a helpful explanation: "Their 'transgressions' rendered some such arrangement as the Mosaic law absolutely necessary, on the supposition that the Messiah was not to appear for a course of ages, and that the revelation of salvation through him was to be preserved in the world by means of the Jewish people."[6] To keep the nation of Israel from the rampant idolatry that surrounded them, God instituted the law.

But, as Paul makes clear, the law was only put in place "until the offspring should come to whom the promise had been made" (3:19). According to God's promise, a descendant would arrive in the line of Abraham's son, Isaac, to bless all the nations. Abraham believed God, and the sons of Abraham are those who believe. The Jews were supposed to live by faith and look to the fulfillment of the promise. They were to seek to obey God as an expression of their faith. They were to offer sacrifices when they transgressed the law. And they were to understand that the function of the law would pass away with the coming of the promised one—Christ.

The law doesn't contradict the promise (3:21–26)
Third, Paul tells them that the law isn't contrary to the promise (3:21). Rather, it serves a twofold purpose.

First, it acts as a *guard* until the fulfillment of the promise (3:22–23). "Before faith came," the Jews were held "captive" under the law. The OT saints looked forward to Christ's coming, and the law kept them within the compass of their duty. But now that "the coming faith" has been revealed, there's no longer any need for the law.

Second, the law acts as a *guide* until the fulfillment of the promise (3:24–25). It was in force for an interim period in salvation history. During that time, it served as a guardian—preparing for, and pointing to, Christ.[7] Now

---

[5] For the reference to "angels," see Acts 7:38, 53; Hebrews 2:2. God gave the promise directly to Abraham, but indirectly through intermediaries (i.e., angels and Moses) to Israel.
[6] Brown, *Galatians*, 151.
[7] See Romans 3:20; 5:20–21; 7:7–8.

that Christ (the "faith") has come, the law has passed away. John Brown summarizes as follows: "The necessary imperfection of the revelation of the method of salvation, till the Saviour appeared and finished his work, and the corresponding limitation of the dispensation of divine influence, rendered such a restrictive system absolutely requisite; but the cause having been removed, the effect must cease."[8]

Conclusion

Paul's main point in this discussion is obvious: if the coming of faith frees Jewish believers from the law, then it's folly to suggest that believing Gentiles should be in bondage to it.

What do I want us to take away from these verses? First, we should be amazed by the unfolding of God's plan of redemption. God promised that the seed of the woman would crush the head of the serpent. God promised Abraham that his seed would bring blessing to the nations. God promised David that his seed would establish an eternal and universal kingdom. Christ is the promised seed.[9] He stands at the centre of redemptive history.

Second, we should be convinced of the important role the law plays in showing us our sin. A young man asks Christ, "Good teacher, what must I do to inherit eternal life?" (Mark 10:17). He responds: "No one is good except God alone. You know the commandments." Christ proceeds to mentions six. The young man makes a bold claim: "Teacher, all these I have kept from my youth." You see, he's working with a deficient view of God's law. And so, Christ responds, "You lack one thing: go, sell all that you have and give to the poor, and you will have treasure in heaven; and come, follow me." With these words Christ forces the young man to take a second look at the law—particularly the tenth commandment. He brings him face to face with his covetousness. The inference is obvious: if he's broken the tenth commandment, then he's broken the first commandment, meaning he doesn't love God with all his heart, soul, mind, and strength. In a word, he's an idolater. That's all the law does. It functions like an x-ray, exposing us for what we truly are.

Third, we should be humbled by the extent of our sin. This is unpleasant, but necessary. It's possible to interpret the law externally and superficially until we reach the tenth commandment. It specifically forces us into the

---

[8] Brown, *Galatians*, 176.
[9] See Genesis 3:15; 17:19; 21:12; 2 Samuel 7:12–14; Psalm 89:3–4; Matthew 1:1.

realm of the heart. It shows us that we separate the gift from the Giver. Consequently, we attach our happiness to people, possessions, and experiences. God's law declares, "You shall not covet." Many of us assure ourselves that we don't covet. But what do we dream about it? What stirs envy in us? What stirs bitterness in us? What circumstances do we think need to change for us to be content? Our answers to such questions show us that God is not on the throne of our hearts. The law breaks sin down into its most basic element: we're idolatrous.

Fourth, we should be convinced of our need of Christ. One of the greatest obstacles to salvation is ignorance of sin. Christ rebukes the church of Laodicea: "You say, I am rich, I have prospered, and I need of nothing, not realizing that you are wretched, pitiable, poor, blind, and naked" (Rev. 3:17). This is the condition of most people. They regard sin light-heartedly because they regard God's law light-heartedly.

Fifth, we should be overwhelmed by God's grace. The fact that the gospel is a promise calls our attention to God's grace as opposed to our effort. God's promise is made to Abraham's offspring, Christ, and by consequence to those who are one with him. Christ was elected, and we in him. Christ was crucified, and we in him. Christ was resurrected, and we in him. Christ was glorified, and we in him. Christ is the heir of all things, and we in him.

Sixth, we should be encouraged by what it means to be a son of God. We're sons of God through faith in Christ (3:26). God is a universal Creator, Sovereign, Judge, and King, but he isn't a universal Father. In Christ alone we approach God as our reconciled Father. He isn't a terrifying God but a loving God. He isn't a condemning God but a pardoning God. Our peace with God is such that he loves us as if we had never been the object of his wrath. He is our Father.

10
Baptized into Christ (3:27–29)

How do we see ourselves? There are only two options on the table. According to the first, our chief identity is determined by something about us—perhaps our nationality or ethnicity; perhaps our school or career; perhaps our role as husband, wife, father, or mother; perhaps a team, hobby, sport, cause, or skill; perhaps a relationship or experience.

When our chief identity is determined by something about us, it inevitably leads to problems. If it's determined by our role as a husband or wife, what happens when this role changes or ends? If it's determined by our nationality or ethnicity, what happens when we meet people who are different from us? If it's determined by our skills and abilities, what happens when others don't appreciate us? If it's determined by our causes and opinions, what happens when others disagree with us? If it's determined by our accomplishments, what happens when we fail? If it's determined by our appearance, what happens when we meet someone who's better looking than us? If it's determined by our job or school, what happens when we interact with those less skilled or less educated than us? If it's determined by our standards, what happens when others don't measure up? If it's determined by our children, what happens when they let us down or embarrass us? If it's determined by our intelligence, what happens when others don't listen to us?

Are you beginning to see how important this is? If we derive our chief identity from something about us, sooner or later we'll encounter disappointment, frustration, resentment, or discouragement.

The second option is to define ourselves according to who we are in Christ. In other words, it's to define ourselves *vertically*. When we do, it shapes everything. It humbles us and causes us to think of others more highly than ourselves. It strengthens us to endure and embrace suffering. It empowers us to serve selflessly and faithfully. It engenders gentleness, meekness, patience, compassion, and kindness. It enables us to extend forgiveness when others have wronged us. Embracing our identity in Christ is foundational to everything.

In 3:27, Paul tells us that to be a believer is to be "baptized into Christ." Christ takes hold of us by the Holy Spirit, and we take hold of him by faith. These two bind us together, whereby we become one. We're "baptized" (plunged) with the Spirit into Christ's body. This is our identity. Paul goes on to highlight three implications.

We "have put on Christ" (3:27)

We use the expression "put on" in reference to clothing. Clothing (at the very least, uniforms) tells us a great deal about a person—where they live, work, or study. It's easy to identity some people by their clothing—a policeman, nurse, or pilot. Paul's point is that we're clothed with Christ, meaning he becomes our identity.

The Bible tells us that, in their state of innocence, Adam and Eve were naked and unashamed (Gen. 2:25). But what happened? They disobeyed God's command and, as a result, their conscience began to scream at the top of its lungs. They were overcome with shame, and they tried to hide it by sewing fig leaves into garments (Gen. 3:7). What did God do? "The LORD God made for Adam and for his wife garments of skins and clothed them" (Gen. 3:21). There are two important details in this verse.

First, God made garments of skins for Adam and Eve. This is the first reference in the Bible to substitutionary death. Later, the patriarchs offer sacrifices. Still later, the Israelites offer sacrifices. From the death of these animals, we learn that "without shedding of blood there is no forgiveness" (Heb. 9:22). These sacrifices point to the need for a substitutionary death to atone for our sin. They point to Christ: "the lamb of God, who takes away the sin of the world" (John 1:29).

Second, God clothed Adam and Eve with the garments of skins. In so doing, he covered their shame. This detail transports us to Calvary, where Christ hung naked upon the cross, bearing our shame. He was stripped of his garments that we might be clothed with his righteousness. We can't hide our guilt and shame, nor can we cleanse our conscience. God must clothe us with his Son. "And because of him you are in Christ Jesus, who became to us wisdom from God, righteousness and sanctification and redemption" (1 Cor. 1:30). In other words, all that's necessary to make us eternally happy, content, satisfied, and blessed is found in Christ.

Nothing can my sin erase;
Nothing but the blood of Jesus!
Naught of works, 'tis all of grace;
Nothing but the blood of Jesus![1]

We "are all one in Christ" (3:28)
God doesn't merely save isolated individuals but creates a new humanity. In Colossians 2:19, Paul says that the body is "knit together through its joints and ligaments." Our bodies are full of joints—one bone fitting into another. Both surfaces are smooth, so that they work effortlessly and harmoniously. Ligaments connect bones to bones. Tendons connect bones to muscles. This is how the body is held together. Throughout the body, there's a nervous system. The smallest nerve in my fingertip connects to larger nerves that run through my arm into my spinal cord, where they're connected by strands of nerves to my brain. I initiate movement by willing it in my brain. My brain sends out energy that passes through my nervous system, which then moves my finger, hand, arm, etc. This is how the body functions. Interestingly, in Colossians 2:19, Paul is speaking of Christ's spiritual body—the church.

Our identity in Christ's body necessarily transcends all distinctions (3:28). It's true of ethnicity: there's neither Jew nor Greek. It's true of social status: there's neither slave nor free. It's true of gender: there's neither male nor female. That isn't to say that there are no distinctions in the new humanity, but that they're irrelevant for full participation in it. The only criterion is our relationship with Christ who is "all, and in all" (Col. 3:11).

How significant was this truth for Paul's audience? These were the three greatest fault lines within the Galatian churches: Jew/Gentile; free/slave; male/female. The Jew looked down on the Gentile, the free looked down on the slave, and the male looked down on the female. In a single stroke of the pen, however, Paul turns their world completely upside down. He declares that the foundation of our relationships is our baptism into Christ's body.

We're to preserve the unity of the body (Eph. 4:3). We aren't to tolerate moral or doctrinal evil in our midst. Neither are we to tolerate disputes which arise from envy, bitterness, and misunderstanding. "Let each of you look not only to his own interests, but also to the interests of others" (Phil. 2:3-4). We're to prefer to serve others rather than be served by them. We're to give our attention to how we can help others rather than be helped by them.

---

[1] Robert Lowry, "What Can Wash Away My Sin?" (hymn).

We're to contribute to the growth of the body (Eph. 4:15-16). Because of our union with Christ, we're knit together like joints, ligaments, and tendons in his spiritual body. When each of us functions properly, the body "builds itself up in love." The Holy Spirit distributes gifts to this end. Are we using our gifts to contribute to the growth of this body? Are we functioning properly? As we do, we "grow up in every way into him who is the head" (Eph. 4:13). That's maturity. As a result, we become Christ's visible form in the world, reflecting his splendor, manifesting his glory, displaying his beauty, and mirroring his holiness.

We're to welcome all within the body (Rom. 14:1-3). An obvious consequence of Adam's fall has been the disruption of human society. Because of sin, humanity is full of "envy," "strife," and "malice" (Rom. 1:29-32), and full of "hate" (Titus 3:3). This hatred has many manifestations—one of the most prevalent being prejudice. The term "prejudice" comes from the Latin *praejudicium*, meaning "to decide beforehand." Simply put, it is to despise, mistreat, or belittle others based on preconceived notions concerning their culture, ethnicity, appearance, class, education, or any other factor. Ethnic prejudice (or, racism), specifically, is the use of words, actions, or attitudes, which denigrate others based on preconceived biases regarding their ethnicity.[2] The gospel is the only solution for the sin of prejudice. It reveals that the problem is much deeper than any of us imagine; it's rooted in a depraved heart. And it proposes a solution that's far more radical than any of us imagine because it leaves us without any claim but one: "Christ is all, and in all" (Col. 3:11). The foundation of our relationships is our baptism into Christ, meaning we're Christians before we're anything else. Out of this new identity, we seek to "honor everyone" (1 Pet. 2:17) and "show perfect courtesy toward all people" (Titus 3:2).

We "are Abraham's offspring, heirs according to promise" (3:29)

In this single phrase, Paul sums up his chief point in the third chapter. We can state it as follows. (1) Christ is Abraham's offspring. (2) Therefore, Christ obtains everything that God promised to Abraham. (3) We're baptized into Christ, meaning we're one with him through faith. (4) Therefore, we're Abraham's offspring in Christ. (5) Therefore, we're heirs of everything that God promised to Abraham.

---

[2] J. Manickam, "Racism," in *Dictionary of Mission Theology*, ed. John Corrie (Downers Grove: InterVarsity, 2007), 326

We inherit a renewed body and soul (Rom. 8:23). At the resurrection, God will miraculously gather the scattered molecules of our decayed bodies and fashion them into new imperishable bodies. We'll be glorious in body; we'll have a glorified body like Christ's (Phil. 3:21). They'll be our bodies, but they'll be so much better. We'll also be glorious in soul; we'll be partakers of the divine nature, that is, divine virtues and qualities (2 Peter 1:4).

We inherit a renewed heaven and earth. "For the promise to Abraham and his offspring that he would be heir of the world did not come through the law but through the righteousness of faith" (Rom. 4:13). When did God ever promise Abraham that he would be "heir of the world"? He told him: "I will give to you and to your offspring after you the land of your sojourning, all the land of Canaan, for an everlasting possession" (Gen. 17:8). But how did Abraham understand this promise? "By faith he went to live in the land of promise, as in a foreign land, living in tents with Isaac and Jacob, heirs with him of the same promise. For he was looking forward to the city that has foundations, whose designer and builder is God" (Heb. 11:9-10). Abraham looked to something God would build. He looked to the new heavens and earth as the fulfillment of God's promise.

God gave his promises to Abraham in concepts familiar to him—land. He fulfills his promises, in accordance with the cosmic significance of Christ's redemptive work (Col. 1:15-18). And so, God's covenant with Abraham includes three things: offspring, blessing, and land. There was a material fulfillment of these promises in the history of the nation of Israel (1 Kgs. 4:21). However, the promises pointed beyond the immediate fulfillment to the ultimate fulfillment—Christ. The offspring is Christ and all who believe in him. The blessing is the gospel. The land is the renewed heaven and earth.[3] In Christ we regain the inheritance we lost in Adam.

Conclusion

This, then, is our identity—we've been "baptized into Christ" (3:27). We might be rich or poor, sick or healthy. We might be having a good day or a bad day. We might be feeling great or terrible. There's no change in our relationship to God in Christ. If he loved me yesterday, he loves me today, and he'll love me tomorrow. This is the sum and substance of all the promises: "I will be their God, and they shall be my people" (Jer.

---

[3] See Psalm 37:9, 11, 22, 29, 34; Matthew 5:5.

31:33). This promise is what Christ has purchased for us: "For Christ also suffered once for sins, the righteous for the unrighteous, that he might bring us to God" (1 Pet. 3:18).

11
The Offspring of Abraham (4:1–7)

Imagine for a moment that you're adopting a child. As you meet with the social worker in the last stage of the process, you're told that this twelve-year-old has been in and out of psychotherapy since he was three. He persists in attempting to burn things and skin kittens alive. His father, grandfather, and great-grandfather had histories of violence, ranging from spousal abuse to murder. Each ended his life the same way—suicide. Think for a minute. Would you want this child? ... Well, this child is you, and he's me. That's what the gospel is telling us. Our birth father has fangs. And left to ourselves, we'll show ourselves to be just as serpentine as he is.[1]

According to J.I. Packer, the doctrine of adoption is the "climax of the Bible."[2] There is nothing more encouraging than this: God takes radically depraved sinners into his family and claims them as his sons.[3]

Before considering the significance of this doctrine, it's important to see where we are in the flow of Paul's argument. In a section, stretching from 3:1 to 5:12, Paul seeks to settle the debate over the identity of the sons of Abraham. Who are they? And who are the true heirs of the Abrahamic promise? Some in the churches of Galatia argue that only those who observe the OT law are sons of Abraham and heirs of the promise. Paul strongly disagrees. We can summarize his argument to this point as follows. (1) God justified Abraham on account of his faith. (2) God promised Abraham that the nations would be blessed in the same way. (3) God declared that this promise would find its fulfillment in Abraham's offspring. (4) God gave the law to Moses to serve as a guard and guide until the fulfillment of the promise. (5) Christ is the fulfillment of the promise. (6) The law is no longer needed. (7) Those

---

[1] Russell Moore, *Adopted for Life: The Priority of Adoption for Christian Families and Churches* (Wheaton: Crossway, 2015), 29.

[2] J.I. Packer, *Knowing God* (London: Hodder and Stoughton, 1973), 202.

[3] I unpack this wonderful doctrine in J. Stephen Yuille, *A Hope Deferred: Adoption & the Fatherhood of God* (Wapwallopen: Shepherd Press, 2013).

who believe are the true sons of Abraham. (8) Those who insist on placing themselves under the law are cursed.

Some in the churches of Galatia insist upon performing "the works of the law" for justification. Paul reveals their error by clarifying what Scripture says about (1) the blessing of Abraham (3:6-14), (2) the priority of Abraham (3:15-26), and (3) the offspring of Abraham (3:27-4:7). We've considered the first two, and so here we turn our attention the third.[4]

Illustration (4:1-2)

Paul appeals to an example from everyday life: the relationship between a father and his son. He wants his readers to notice three things. (1) The son is "the heir" and "the owner" of everything that belongs to his father (4:1). (2) The father appoints "the date" when his son will be permitted to make his own decisions (4:2). (3) The father appoints "guardians and managers" to supervise his son until the appointed date (4:2). (4) Until then, the son is "no different from a slave," meaning he isn't free to do as he pleases (4:2).

Application (4:3-5)

Paul applies the illustration to redemptive history. His intention isn't to apply every detail, but to ensure that we grasp the significance of what it means to reach the age of maturity. We can sum up his argument in four points. (1) There was a time when OT believers were "children" (4:3). (2) They were "enslaved to the elementary principles of the world" (4:3). This means that they were under a guardianship (including an "elementary" method of instruction)—namely, the OT law. (3) The "fullness of time" has come (4:4).[5] This means that a new period in salvation history was made a reality by Christ's coming into the world. The law was an era in salvation history marked by immaturity. It was imperfect and incomplete, and it served to prepare for another age. (4) Christ has redeemed "those who were under the law that they might receive adoption as sons" (4:6). With Christ's coming into the world, the appointed time of guardianship has ended, and the OT law has been made obsolete. We have reached the state of maturity that belongs to adopted sons. The term *maturity* "describes not the state of saints as

---

[4] The threefold division of these verses (illustration, application, and implication) is suggested by Schreiner in *Galatians*, 263.

[5] See Mark 1:15; 1 Corinthians 10:11; Ephesians 1:10.

opposed to that of sinners, but the state of saints under the Christian dispensation in contrast with that of saints under the Mosaic dispensation."[6]

Implication (4:6–7)

"And because you are sons, God has sent the Spirit of his Son into our hearts, crying, 'Abba! Father!' So you are no longer a slave, but a son, and if a son, then an heir through God."[7] Christ promised that the Holy Spirit would be "in" us (John 14:17). This is such a certainty that Paul writes, "Anyone who does not have the Spirit of Christ does not belong to him" (Rom 8:9). This doesn't mean that the Holy Spirit changes places from *outside* of us to *inside* of us. Rather, it means that he manifests his presence by his operation in a way that he didn't formerly. It includes his works of regeneration, sanctification, illumination, and inclination. In addition, he guarantees our inheritance (Eph 1:14); he intercedes on our behalf (Rom 8:26); he strengthens us to grow in our appreciation of Christ's love (Eph. 3:16–17); and he fills us so that we live in such a way as to glorify Christ (Eph. 5:18–21).

Because of his influence in our hearts, the Holy Spirit causes us to cry: "Abba! Father!" He makes truth come alive to us: "Christ died for sinners; God welcomes sinners who come to him through faith in Christ; I'm a sinner; I believe in Christ; therefore, I'm a child of God!" In this way, the Holy Spirit makes our relationship with God real to us.

God has placed us in his family; however, there are two realities to salvation: *now* and *not yet*. We live with the tension of being caught between these two realities. We're saved, yet we await salvation. We're redeemed, yet we await redemption. We're adopted, yet we await adoption. Salvation is inaugurated, but it isn't consummated. It's all ours, but we haven't yet entered the full enjoyment of it. We know we will because we have the Holy Spirit—the pledge. And thus, we cry, "Abba! Father!"

Conclusion

"In love he predestined us for adoption through Jesus Christ, according to the purpose of his will" (Eph. 1:5). Paul stresses the fact that Christ is the means through which God adopts us. He's thinking primarily of his substitutionary death. Christ declares, "For even the Son of Man came not to be served but to serve, and to give his life as a ransom for many" (Mark 10:45).

---

[6] Brown, *Galatians*, 192.
[7] See Romans 8:17.

In the original language, the preposition *for* is *anti*. It literally means *instead of*. The term *ransom* means to purchase the freedom of a slave. And so, Christ is saying that he gives his life for us to free us. Our bondage is immeasurable in magnitude. Therefore, the ransom must be infinite in measure—the very Son of God.

When Christ died on the cross as our substitute, he accomplished two things for us. First, he paid our debt. We're guilty of disobeying God, and we're guilty of breaking his covenant. As a result, we're debtors to him—under the curse. But Christ paid our debt upon the cross. That's called *redemption*.

Second, Christ purchased our inheritance. At the time of Adam's fall, we lost everything. Most importantly, we fell into a state of alienation from God. But Christ purchased our inheritance (membership in God's family) upon the cross. That's called *adoption*. In Christ, we possess a new name, new position, and new identity. And Christ passes on this inheritance in perpetuity to all his people.

It's important to note that the link between redemption and adoption is reconciliation: a change in our legal status before God. By Christ's death, redemption effects reconciliation (peace with God), and reconciliation becomes the basis of God's adoption of us. Paul describes this double-work (redemption and adoption) in very clear terms in our text: "But when the fullness of time had come, God sent forth his Son, born of a woman, born under the law, to redeem those who were under the law, so that we might receive adoption as son" (4:4–5).

As adopted sons, we're dearly loved. God provides for us (Matt. 6:26), welcomes us into his presence (Eph. 3:12), watches over us (Rom. 8:28), and guards us (1 Pet. 1:5). "He knows our frame; he remembers that we are dust" (Ps. 103:14). God treats us as his "only" sons.

As adopted sons, we can trust God with the details of our lives. His wisdom isn't man's wisdom, and his ways aren't man's ways (Rom. 11:33). He isn't a distant tyrant; rather, he has entered history, assumed humanity, and suffered for us. He has our best interests before him. His plan is best.

As adopted sons, we can wait patiently for the promised inheritance. "If we hope for what we do not see, we wait for it with patience" (Rom. 8:25). Hope is fixed on the return of Christ, the resurrection from the dead, the full and final deliverance from sin, and the renovation of the entire cosmos. Hope makes this future certainty a present reality. This is a light that penetrates the shadows. It's immune to every illness, every threat, every grief, every worry, every challenge, and every loss. It reminds us that the best is yet to come.

God's Word is full of comfort, but there are two truths "which are the greatest support of the heart under any trouble—adoption and particular providence."[8] We need to savour the sweetness of this single statement: God is our Father. If our mind is troubled, we need to think on this. Here's stability amid societal decay, financial woes, health problems, and broken relationships. If our heart is troubled, we need to think on this. Here's strength for enduring difficulty, trust for facing uncertainty, and peace for overcoming anxiety. If our conscience is troubled, we need to think on this. Here's assurance that God welcomes me (a penitent sinner) because of Christ (a sufficient Saviour). We are the sons of God.

> Behold, what love, what boundless love,
> The Father hath bestowed
> On sinners lost, that we should be
> Now called the sons of God![9]

---

[8] Manton, *Works*, 7:331.
[9] Robert Bowell, "What Manner of Love" (hymn).

12
A Triune Being (4:4–7)

As Augustine was walking by the seashore one day, contemplating the doctrine of the Trinity, he stopped to observe a small boy running back and forth from the water's edge to a place on the beach. The boy was carrying water from the sea in a shell and pouring it into a hole in the sand. Augustine asked, "My boy, what are doing?" "I am trying to bring all the sea into this hole," the boy replied. "But that is impossible, my dear child, the hole cannot contain all that water." Fixing his gaze upon Augustine, the boy declared, "It is no more impossible than what you are trying to do—comprehend the mystery of the Trinity with your small intelligence."[1]

To some extent, we all struggle with rationalism. We assume we should be able to explain everything, including God. But we can't fully comprehend the One who is incomprehensible (Rom. 11:33). The bounded cannot grasp the boundless. The limited cannot fathom the limitless. "Great is the LORD, and greatly to be praised, and his greatness is unsearchable" (Ps. 145:3). In a word, our God is infinite. When used in reference to him, the term "infinity" doesn't have a mathematical connotation. Instead, it speaks of his transcendence—the reality that he's free from all limitations.

God is infinite in relation to *being*. We refer to this as *aseity*, meaning God has life from himself (*a se*). "As the Father has life in himself, so he has granted the Son also to have life in himself" (John 5:26). "The God who made the world and all things in it, since he is Lord of heaven and earth, does not dwell in temples made with hands; nor is he served by human hands, as though he needed anything" (Acts 17:24–25). God is completely self-existent and self-sufficient.

God is also infinite in relation to *space*. We refer to this as *ubiquity*, meaning God is omnipresent. God is "over all and through all and in all" (Eph. 4:6). He's always present in all places yet restricted to none. "'Am I a God

---

[1] This popular story is undoubtedly apocryphal. It was first told by Jacobus de Voragine, Archbishop of Genoa, in 1275. Despite its dubious origins, its point is well made.

who is near ... and not a God far off? Can a man hide himself in hiding places so I do not see him? Do I not fill the heavens and the earth?" (Jer. 23:23–24).

God is also infinite in relation to *time*. We refer to this as his *eternality*, meaning God is above all succession of time. He's without *beginning*: "Your throne is established from of old; You are from everlasting" (Ps. 93:2). He's without *ending*: "They will perish, but you will remain; they will all wear out like a garment. You will change them like a robe, and they will pass away, but you are the same, and your years have no end" (Ps. 102:26–27).

God is free from all limitations in relation to being, space, and time. In sum, he is eternal Creator. His act of creation is eternal because time begins with creation; that is to say, the creation of the universe isn't a moment that follows another moment. This is of utmost importance when it comes to our understanding of God. Simply put, God is beyond the created universe, including time and space. He knows "no past or present," but remains in "the same indivisible point of eternity."[2] This means he is *perfect being*. Because he is self-existent, he's self-sufficient. Because he's self-sufficient, he's all sufficient. "Can you find out the deep things of God? Can you find out the limit of the Almighty?" (Job 11:7). No, you can't, nor can I! We must keep God's unsearchable greatness in view when we ponder the doctrine of the Trinity. The finite cannot comprehend the infinite.

For this reason, we must stay close to God's Word. When we do, we learn that "God is one" (3:20).[3] We also learn that "when the fullness of time had come" the one God "sent forth his Son" (4:4) and "sent the Spirit of his Son" (4:6). These historical *sendings* (known as the incarnation and Pentecost) reveal that the Son and the Spirit are eternal. After all, it's only possible to send that which already exists. The Son and the Spirit exist prior to the time they were sent. Why is this significant? It means that God behaves as the Father, the Son, and the Spirit in time precisely because he is the Father, the Son, and the Spirit in eternity (beyond time).[4]

---

[2] Manton, *Works*, 4:114.
[3] See Deuteronomy 4:35; 6:4; Psalm 86:10; Isaiah 45:21; 46:9; 1 Corinthians 8:4; 1 Timothy 2:5.
[4] Fred Sanders, *The Triune God* (Grand Rapids: Zondervan, 2016), 112–113.

Processions

For starters, the Son is sent in time because he stands in an eternal relation of origin with the Father.[5] This is called *eternal generation*. The Son isn't eternally generated by the Father *out of* the divine essence, but *within* the one divine essence; that is, the person of the Father begets the person of the Son. It doesn't happen in time, nor is it an act of creation. This relation is who they are: the Son is "the only begotten of [from] the Father" (John 1:14).[6]

Similarly, the Spirit is sent in time because he stands in an eternal relation of origin with the Father and the Son.[7] This is called *eternal spiration*. Christ declares, "And I will ask the Father, and he will give you another Helper, to be with you forever, even the Spirit of truth" (John 14:16-17).[8] Later, he adds, "But when the Helper comes, whom I will send to you from the Father, the Spirit of truth, who proceeds from the Father, he will bear witness about me" (John 15:26). In these verses Christ clearly distinguishes between his sending of the Spirit and the Spirit's proceeding from the Father. The latter is a description of the Spirit's continuous relation with the Father. The Spirit doesn't go forth from God's essence but proceeds within God's essence as an internal act of the Father and the Son.

It has been said that "the doctrine of the Trinity stands or falls with the right understanding of the relations in God."[9] In other words, we must distinguish between the one divine essence (or substance) and the eternal relations that each person has with the others in God. If we don't, we will end up falling into one of two errors. The first is *modalism*, whereby we blur the distinctions of the three eternal relations. The second is *subordinationism*, whereby we create a hierarchy among the three eternal relations. Subordination does exist in God's work of redemption: the Father sends the Son, and then both the Father and the Son send the Spirit. However, this subordination in redemption doesn't reflect any subordination within God. The term *Son* doesn't denote subordination, but likeness. The term *Spirit* doesn't denote subordination, but activity. The Father, the Son, and the Spirit are co-

---

[5] For the relationship between the Father and the Son, see John 8:42; 10:30; 15:18-30; 17:1-26.

[6] See John 1:18; 3:16-18; 1 John 4:9.

[7] For the relationship between the Father, the Son, and the Spirit, see John 14:16-18; 15:26; 16:7-15.

[8] Also see John 14:26-27.

[9] Sanders, *The Triune God*, 35.

eternal and co-equal—one in substance, power, wisdom, will, and life. God is "one" (3:20).

Christ affirmed this very thing: "I and the Father are one" (John 10:30). The verb is plural, meaning the Father and Son are distinct. Yet the predicate is singular and neuter, "I and the Father are one thing," thereby indicating that the Father and the Son are the same. As Christ affirms elsewhere, the Father is in the Son and the Son is in the Father (John 17:21-22).[10] Therefore, to receive the Son is the receive the Father (John 13:20); to hate the Son is to hate the Father (John 15:23); to honour the Son is to honour the Father (John 5:23); to know the Son is to know the Father (John 14:7; 16:3; 17:3); to see the Son is to see the Father (John 12:45; 14:9); and to believe in the Son is to believe in the Father (John 14:1).

Based on the testimony of Scripture, therefore, we confess that God is triune—he is three (*tri*) eternal relations in one (*une*) being. Thus, "we worship one God in trinity and trinity in unity, without either confusing the persons or dividing the substance ... Thus the Father is God, the Son is God, the Spirit is God; and yet there are not three Gods, but there is one God."[11]

Implications

When we speak of the "one God" as existing in three eternal relations (the Father, the Son, and the Spirit), we aren't being academically picky or theologically fussy. We're proclaiming the very heart of the Christian faith. How so? We affirm, "God is love" (1 John 4:8), but this statement is meaningless divorced from the doctrine of the Trinity. As C. S. Lewis states, "All sorts of people are fond of repeating the Christian statement that 'God is love.' But they seem not to notice that the words 'God is love' have no real meaning unless God contains at least two persons. Love is something that one person has for another person. If God was a single person, then before the world was made, he was not love."[12] All that to say, God is love precisely because he's triune.

You see, our understanding of God doesn't begin with his identity as "Creator" or "Ruler" or even "Redeemer" because these things require creation. Our God is above creation. He's infinite—beyond all spatial and

---

[10] See John 1:1, 18; 10:30, 38; 14:10, 20; 16:32.

[11] "The Athanasian Creed," in *The Creeds of Christendom*, 3 vols., ed. Philip Schaff (Grand Rapids: Baker Books, 1998), 1:35-37.

[12] C.S. Lewis, *Mere Christianity* (San Francisco: Harper, 2015), 160.

temporal limitations. Therefore, our understanding of God must move beyond creation to his chief identity. Which is what? He's Father.[13] This is who he is *eternally*.

Here's the wonder of wonders: "The Father so delights in his eternal love for the Son that he desires to share it with all who will believe. Ultimately, the Father sent the Son because the Father so loved the Son—and wanted to share that love and fellowship. His love for the world is the overflow of his almighty love for his Son."[14] To sum up, the Father loves us (1 John 3:1); the Son reveals the Father's love (Eph. 5:2); and the Spirit assures us of the Father's love (Rom. 5:5). As Paul declares in our text, "But when the fullness of time had come, God sent forth his Son, born of woman, born under the law, to redeem those who were under the law, so that we might receive adoption as sons. And because you are sons, God has sent the Spirit of his Son into our hearts, crying, 'Abba! Father!'" (4:4–7).

Conclusion

It is this doctrine that distinguishes Christianity from all other religions. We often hear people say that all religions should focus on what they have in common. As Christians, we don't share anything in common with other religions. We hold to an absolute—namely, there's only one God who is the Father, the Son, and the Holy Spirit.

This is an *essential* truth. Our salvation rests upon it. Peter says we're "elect ... according to the foreknowledge of God the Father, in the sanctification of the Spirit, for obedience to Jesus Christ and for sprinkling with his blood" (1 Pet. 1:1–2). Therefore, we praise the Father for choosing us, the Son for redeeming us, and the Spirit for sanctifying us. We praise God triune for the eternal covenant of redemption whereby the Father, the Son, and the Spirit accomplish our salvation.

This is an *exceptional* truth. The knowledge of it is blessedness. How so? God gives us himself (blessedness) by giving us his Son and his Spirit (4:4–7). Salvation, therefore, is receiving the Son and the Spirit. We relate to the one God who is the Father, the Son, and the Spirit (1 John 1:3). As Augustine writes, "The true objects of enjoyment, then, are the Father and the Son and

---

[13] See Exodus 4:22; Deuteronomy 1:31; 8:5; Psalm 103:13; Jeremiah 3:19; Isaiah 63:16; 64:8; John 20:17; 1 Corinthians 1:3; 8:6; 1 Peter 1:3; Hebrews 12:7.

[14] Michael Reeves, *Delighting in the Trinity: An Introduction to the Christian Faith* (Downers Grove: InterVarsity Press, 2012), 70.

the Holy Spirit, who are at the same time the Trinity, one being, supreme above all, and common to all who enjoy him."[15]

As John Owen explains, our communion with the Father is especially in love (2 Cor. 13:14; Rom. 5:8; 1 John 4:9–10). The Father's love "is the fountain from whence all other sweetnesses flow."[16] We respond to his love by loving him and others (Eph. 4:32–5:2). Our communion with the Son is especially in grace (2 Cor. 13:14; John 1:14–16; Rom. 3:24). Grace isn't merely a gift sent from Christ, but the blessings of union with Christ (Eph. 1:3). We respond to his grace by walking with him in faith (Col. 2:6–7). Our communion with the Spirit is especially in fellowship (2 Cor. 13:14). He's the living bond who brings together God's people into one temple. He dwells in us so that the Father's love and the Son's grace are realized in our lives (John 14:17, 23). We respond by cherishing this fellowship and avoiding anything that grieves him (Eph. 4:1–3, 29–32).

In sum, "Knowing God is the heart of our spiritual experience as Christians, and the God whom we have come to know is a Trinity of three coequal persons, revealed to us as the Father, the Son, and the Holy Spirit."[17]

> Praise God, from whom all blessings flow;
> Praise him, all creatures here below;
> Praise him above, ye heav'nly host;
> Praise Father, Son, and Holy Ghost!
>
> Praise God the Father who's the source;
> Praise God the Son who is the course;
> Praise God the Spirit who's the flow;
> Praise God, our portion here below![18]

---

[15] Augustine, *On Christian Doctrine*, 1:5, in *Nicene and Post-Nicene Fathers*, vol 2, ed. Philipp Schaff (Peabody: Hendrickson, 1990).

[16] Owen, *Works*, 2:22.

[17] Gerald Bray, "Union and Communion: Joining the Fellowship of Heaven," in *For All the Saints: Evangelical Theology and Christian Spirituality*, eds. Timothy George and Alister McGrath (Louisville: Westminster John Knox Press, 2003), 109.

[18] Thomas Ken, "Praise God from Whom All Blessings Flow" (hymn).

13
"Born of a Woman" (4:4)

J.I. Packer writes, "Here are two mysteries for the price of one—the plurality of persons within the unity of God, and the union of Godhead and manhood in the person of Jesus."[1] We considered the first of these "mysteries" in the previous chapter; now we turn our attention to the second.

Paul declares that "when the fullness of time had come, God sent forth his Son, born of a woman" (4:4). At the outset of his ministry, Christ announced, "The time is fulfilled, and the kingdom of God is at hand" (Mark 1:14). Obviously, a fulfillment requires a promise. So what promise was Christ talking about? He was declaring that the OT expectation concerning the arrival of God's kingdom was fulfilled. In the days of the patriarchs, this kingdom was promised; in the days of the judges, it was prefigured; in the days of the kings, it was previewed; and in the days of the prophets, it was prophesied. All that to say, God's plan concerning his kingdom was progressively revealed throughout the OT. It came to fruition in "the fullness of time" when God "sent forth his Son."

John describes this moment as follows: "The word became flesh and dwelt among us" (John 1:14). From the context, it's evident that the "word" is an eternal being, actively involved in creation (John 1:1-2). The verb "became" refers to a definitive moment in human history—"the fullness of time." What happened? The "word became flesh"—that is, he became a finite, mortal, human being.

> Veiled in flesh the Godhead see,
> Hail the incarnate Deity!
> Pleased as man with man to dwell,
> Jesus our Emmanuel.[2]

---

[1] Packer, *Knowing God*, 45.
[2] Charles Wesley, "Hark the Herald Angels Sing" (hymn).

We believe that Christ emptied himself

Paul affirms that Christ "was in the form of God" (Phil. 2:6). The term "form" (*morphe*) refers to the essential nature of a person or thing. The "form" of a servant is really a servant (Phil. 2:7), and the "form" of God is really God. In other words, when Paul affirms that Christ "was in the form of God," he's declaring that Christ is God. "He is the blessed and only sovereign, the King of kings and Lord of lords, who alone has immortality, who dwells in unapproachable light, whom no one has ever seen or can see" (1 Tim. 6:15–16). And yet, says Paul, Christ "emptied himself." What does this mean?

In the last chapter, we noted that there are three eternal relations in the one God—the Father, the Son, and the Spirit. The Father sends the Son and the Spirit in time because the Son and the Spirit proceed from the Father in eternity (John 8:42; 15:26). The Father sends the Son (incarnation) because the Son stands in an eternal relation of origin to the Father (eternal generation). The Father and the Son send the Spirit (Pentecost) because the Spirit stands in an eternal relation of origin to the Father and the Son (eternal spiration). It's the Son (Christ) who "emptied himself." The One who "is over all and through all and in all" (Eph. 4:6) was carried in the womb of Mary. He drank milk from his mother, yet he was the Creator of that milk. He grew in wisdom and stature, yet he possessed all knowledge and wisdom. He was hungry and weary, yet he was all-sufficient and self-sufficient.

When he "emptied himself," he didn't cease to be who is (God) but took to himself the very opposite—human nature. He hid his heavenly glory (John 17:5), and he gave up the independent exercise of his authority (John 5:30). He "emptied himself" of these things with reference to his human nature—not his divine nature. As the Creed of Nicaea (AD 325) affirms:

> We believe ... in one Lord Jesus Christ, the Son of God, begotten of the Father, only-begotten, that is, of the substance of the Father, God of God, Light of Light, true God of true God, begotten not made, of one substance with the Father, through whom all things were made, things in heaven and things on the earth; who for us men and for our salvation came down and was made flesh, and became man, suffered, and rose on the third day, ascended into the heavens, is coming to judge living and dead.[3]

---

[3] "The Creed of Nicaea," in *The Creeds of Christendom*, 1:58–59.

The phrase—"the substance (*homoousios*) of the Father"—is extremely significant. The term "substance" is a compound word: *hom* (co) and *ousia* (essence or substance); hence, it literally means "co-essential" or "co-substantial." The term "essence" denotes the totality of qualities which constitute a being. Therefore, by affirming that the Son is "the substance of the Father," we affirm that he is the eternal God, distinct yet equal with the Father.

We believe that Christ assumed the human nature
Christ was conceived of the Holy Spirit (Luke 1:35). This conception was the result of the power of the Most High. The name *Most High* is the superlative of the Greek term for height. In other words, God is the highest: "Behold, heaven and the highest heaven cannot contain you" (1 Kgs. 8:27). The matter (or, substance) in the conception was natural—Mary's egg in Mary's womb. However, the conception itself was supernatural. There was no human father; rather, the Holy Spirit worked upon the substance in Mary's womb, thereby producing Christ's human nature.

At that moment, "the word became flesh" (John 1:14). This doesn't mean that the Son of God changed what he was (and is) but assumed what he was not (human nature). Elsewhere, we read that Christ was "made sin" (2 Cor. 5:21) and "made a curse" (Gal. 3:13). These expressions don't mean he *turned into* sin or a curse. Likewise, the eternal Word didn't turn into a man, so that he lost his essential being; rather, he assumed the human nature.

Christ assumed a human body with all its members (Matt. 4:2; Luke 2:52; 24:38–39; John 4:6; 19:28, 34). And he assumed a human soul with all its faculties. He loves (Mark 10:21; John 11:3; 13:23), pities (Matt. 9:36; 14:14; 15:32; 20:34), grieves (Matt. 26:37; John 11:33, 35, 38), and rejoices (John 15:11; 17:13; Heb. 12:2). He's astonished (Mark 6:6; Luke 7:9), troubled (Mark 14:32–42; John 12:27), and lonely (Mark 15:34). In the words of John Flavel, Christ "assumed the true human nature into the unity of his divine person, with all its integral parts and essential properties; and so was made, or became, a true and real man by that assumption."[4]

---

[4] John Flavel, *Christ and His Threefold Office*, ed. J. Stephen Yuille (Grand Rapids: Reformation Heritage Books, 2021), 36.

We believe that Christ assumed human nature with its sinless infirmities

Paul says that God sent Christ "in the likeness of sinful flesh" (Rom. 8:3). This doesn't imply that Christ's human nature is sinful. On the contrary, "he knew no sin" (2 Cor. 5:21), "he committed no sin" (1 Pet. 2:22), and "in him there is no sin" (1 John 3:5). Christ has the same human nature as us; however, he doesn't have the same fallen human nature as us. His human nature is blameless (Heb. 4:15; 7:26; 9:14). By the expression, "likeness of sinful flesh," Paul means that Christ's human nature had all the negative effects of sin upon it—hunger, thirst, pain, weariness, etc.

We believe that Christ is fully God and fully man

The Council of Chalcedon (AD 451) issued an important statement concerning the person of Christ:

> We, then, following the holy Fathers, all with one consent, teach men to confess one and the same Son, our Lord Jesus Christ, the same perfect in Godhead and also perfect in manhood; truly God and truly man, of a reasonable soul and body; consubstantial with the Father according to the Godhead, and consubstantial with us according to the manhood; in all things like unto us, without sin; begotten before all ages of the Father according to the Godhead, and in these latter days, for us and for our salvation, born of the Virgin Mary, the God-bearer, according to the Manhood; one and the same Christ, Son, Lord, Only-begotten, to be acknowledged, inconfusedly, unchangeably, indivisibly, inseparably; the distinction of natures being by no means taken away by the union, but rather the property of each nature being preserved, and concurring in one Person and one Subsistence, not parted or divided into two persons, but one and the same Son, and only begotten, God the Word, the Lord Jesus Christ, as the prophets from the beginning have declared concerning him, and the Lord Jesus Christ himself has taught us, and the Creed of the holy Fathers has been handed down to us.[5]

This confession sets the boundaries within which we can marvel at the mystery of the incarnation. It postulates five key truths. (1) Christ has two natures, meaning he's fully God and fully man. (2) Each nature remains distinct. His human nature didn't absorb his divine nature, nor did his divine nature absorb his human nature. (3) Christ is one person, meaning his two

---

[5] "The Chalcedon Definition," in *The Creeds of Christendom*, 1:62–63.

natures (while distinct) make but one person. He's the "Christ according to the flesh, who is over all, God blessed forever" (Rom. 9:5). (4) The properties of each nature are ascribed to the person of Christ, yet nothing from the human nature is imparted to the divine nature or vice a versa. (5) What is true of one nature is true of Christ's person. Thus, it's possible to say that "the Lord of glory was crucified" (1 Cor. 2:8), "the blood of God redeemed the church" (Acts 20:28), and Christ was both in heaven and earth at the same time (John 3:13). We can declare, "He who hung the earth is hanging. He who fixed the heavens in place has been fixed in place. He who laid the foundations of the universe has been laid on a tree. The Master has been profaned. God has been murdered."[6]

Conclusion

That is the mystery of the incarnation. An obvious question remains: Why did the Son of God become flesh? Paul tells us: "When the fullness of time had come, God sent forth his Son, born of woman, born under the law, to redeem those who were under the law" (4:4). In other words, the incarnation has a redemptive purpose. Because of our sin, we're cut off from God (Eph. 2:1–3). We stand in need of someone who can bridge the gap between God and us. This "someone" is Christ. "There is one God, and there is one mediator between God and men, the man Christ Jesus, who gave himself as a ransom for all, which is the testimony given at the proper time" (1 Tim. 2:6–7). Christ is fully God, and able to act on his behalf. He's fully man, and able to act on our behalf. Christ (fully God and fully man) stands between the righteous God and the rebellious sinner, bridging the expanse. He redeems us "from the curse of the law by becoming a course for us" (3:13).

Having offered his atoning sacrifice, he now ensures its efficacy by his eternal intercession. "Consequently, he is able to save to the uttermost those who draw near to God through him, since he always lives to make intercession for them" (Heb. 7:25). Christ presents himself before God on behalf of his people (Heb. 9:24), thereby ensuring the application of all that he procured by his crucifixion and resurrection.

Moreover, we now have a high priest who is "able to sympathize with our weaknesses" because he has been "tempted as we are" (Heb. 4:15). Hence, we can "with confidence draw near to the throne of grace" (Heb. 4:16).

---

[6] Melito of Sardis, as quoted in Michael Haykin, *Rediscovering the Church Fathers: Who They Were and How They Shaped the Church* (Wheaton: Crossway, 2011), 21–22.

We're free from a disbelief of acceptance that arises from a sense of our own unworthiness (Rom. 5:1-2; Eph. 3:12). When we draw near, we "receive mercy and find grace to help in time of need" (Heb. 4:16). In other words, we receive assistance to deal with "our weaknesses" (2 Cor. 12:9; Phil. 4:19).

> Before the throne of God above
> I have a strong and perfect plea.
> A great high priest whose name is Love
> Who ever lives and pleads for me.
> My name is graven on his hands,
> My name is written on his heart.
> I know that while in heaven he stands
> No tongue can bid me thence depart.[7]

---

[7] Charitie L. Bancroft, "Before the Throne of God Above" (hymn).

14
Known by God (4:8–20)

In the last two chapters, we've taken time to ponder the two great mysteries of the Christian faith—namely, "the plurality of persons within the unity of God, and the union of Godhead and manhood in the person of Jesus."[1]

We return in this chapter to Paul's main argument. By way of reminder, he's addressing those who think they must observe the OT law to inherit the promised blessing. He makes it clear that they've misunderstood redemptive history. God made a promise to Abraham: "In you shall all the nations be blessed." God established the law (the Mosaic Covenant) until the arrival of the promise—Christ (3:19). The law, therefore, served a temporary purpose. "It was added because of transgressions" (3:19). With the coming of Christ, therefore, it's no longer needed. Paul is explaining this to people who think they must live "under" the OT law. He presents four main arguments to show them the folly of their position.

An Argument from Experience (3:1–5)
"Did you receive the Spirit by works of the law or by hearing with faith?" (3:3)

An Argument from Scripture (3:6–4:7)
"Is the law then contrary to the promise of God?" (3:21)

An Argument from Experience (4:8–20)
"What then has become of the blessing you felt?" (4:15)

An Argument from Scripture (4:21–31)
"Do you not listen to the law?" (4:21)

An Appeal (5:1–12)

Here we turn our attention to Paul's third argument. As in the case of his first argument, he appeals to the Galatians' experience.

---

[1] Packer, *Knowing God*, 45.

The Fullness of Time

Their former condition (4:8)

Paul reminds them that formerly they "did not know God" and they "were enslaved to those that by nature are not gods." The region of Galatia was full of idols, shrines, and temples. Idolatry was prevalent in the home: fathers led their families as they worshiped their household gods. It was prevalent in the guild: tradesmen gathered to worship their patron god and conduct business. It was prevalent in the city: citizens gathered at appointed times for sacrifices, festivals, etc. It was prevalent in the empire: the Romans worshiped the spirit who indwelt the emperor. Idolatry was all the Galatians had ever known. They "were enslaved to those that by nature are not gods."

This is the predicament of the entire human race (Rom. 1:18–32). By nature, man is enslaved to idolatry. These idols might be literal images and statues, or false religions, or false concepts of God. An idol is anything that takes the place of God in our hearts. "Certain it is that many among us practice a spiritual idolatry in their hearts," writes William Perkins. "For look what a man loves most, and cares for most, and delights most in; that is his God."[2]

Their present condition (4:9)

Paul reminds them that they "have come to know God, or rather to be known of God." Clearly, something has changed in their experience. What Paul says of the Thessalonian believers could be said of the Galatian believers: they "turned to God from idols to serve the living and true God" (1 Thess. 1:9). The adjectives "living" and "true" emphasize the difference between God and idols: simply put, idols have neither life nor truth. Conversion is to have the heart's affections turned from idolatry and set upon God alone. Joseph Alleine declares, "[Conversion] cures the fatal misery of the fall by turning the heart from its idol to the living God."[3] This "turning of the heart" is characterized by two tremendous experiences.

Knowing God

First, they "know God." To understand what Paul means, we must differentiate between a *factual* and *relational* knowledge of God. Everyone possesses a *factual* knowledge of God; that is, everyone knows that he's the Creator and that he's all-powerful and all-wise (Rom. 1:19–20). What's the problem?

---

[2] Perkins, *Galatians*, 2:267.
[3] Joseph Alleine, *A Sure Guide to Heaven* (1672; rpt., London: Banner of Truth, 1989), 38.

Man suppresses the truth by his unrighteousness (Rom. 1:18). While the natural man possesses a *factual* knowledge of God, he doesn't possess a *relational* knowledge of God.

To be converted is to know God *relationally*. It isn't merely accepting or affirming certain truths concerning God—although it includes this. Knowing God is more; it's enjoying a relationship with him. When we're converted, we apprehend that God is our Father in Christ (4:6). We possess new affections and inclinations. As a result, we desire to do his will. John declares, "Whoever says, 'I know him' but does not keep his commandments is a liar, and the truth is not in him" (1 John 2:4). Again, "No one who abides in him keeps on sinning; no one who keeps on sinning has either seen him or known him" (1 John 3:6).

Being known by God

Second, they are "known of God." Again, we must be careful to note the difference between *factual* and *relational* knowledge. God knows everyone *factually*, but he doesn't know everyone *relationally*. In the preceding verses, Paul speaks of adoption; thus, to be known by God is to be known as his adopted child. "The Lord knows those who are his" (2 Tim. 2:19). Christ proclaims, "I know my own" (John 10:14). Who are his own? They're those whom the Father "has given" to him (John 17:2, 9, 24). Elsewhere, Christ declares that the sheep hear the shepherd's voice and "he calls his own sheep by name and leads them out" (John 10:3). We must meditate upon this wonderful reality. He knows us "by name." He knows everything about us. He embraces us with a special love. He delights in us and approves of us. He's aware of our needs, tears, fears, struggles, and worries. Being known by God is "the full and final comfort of the believer."[4]

> Jesus, the very thought of thee,
> With sweetness fills my breast.
> But sweeter far thy face to see,
> And in thy presence rest;
> But what to those who find?
> Ah, this, no tongue or pen can show;
> The love of Jesus, what it is,

---

[4] Richard Baxter, *The Practical Works of Rev. Richard Baxter* (London: James Duncan, 1830), 15:285.

None but his loved ones know.⁵

Their danger (4:9-20)

Given their experience—namely, the marked difference between their former condition (they "did not know God") and their present condition (they "have come to know God, or rather to be known by God")—Paul asks a pointed question: "How can you turn back again to the weak and worthless elementary principles of the world, whose slaves you want to be once more? You observe days and months and seasons and years!" Their desire to live under the OT law is absurd. By esteeming the law as a meritorious cause of salvation, they're exchanging one type of bondage (paganism) for another (Judaism). John Brown remarks, "While they were Gentiles, they performed a set of useless ceremonies in honour of their false deities; and now they do the same thing, though unintentionally, in honour of the true God."⁶

As a result of their folly, Paul laments, "I am afraid I may have labored over you in vain" (4:11). He desperately wants them to come to their senses. "Brothers, I entreat you, become as I am, for I also have become as you are" (4:12). He has escaped enslavement to the OT law; in particular, he has escaped those laws that limit interaction between Jews and Gentiles. He has become like them—a Gentile. Now, he commands them to become like him. He wants them to imitate his example in terms of his relationship to the OT law. And so, how does he proceed?

An appeal

"You did me no wrong. You know it was because of a bodily ailment that I preached the gospel to you at first, and though my condition was a trial to you, you did not scorn or despise me, but received me as an angel of God, as Christ Jesus" (4:12-14). We don't know what ailed Paul when he preached in Galatia.⁷ His purpose in mentioning his ailment is to remind the recipients of his letter that his weakness could have been an impediment to the proclamation of the gospel. After all, who would believe that someone so afflicted could be a messenger of God? But rather than reject him, they had "received" him as Christ Jesus.

---

⁵ Bernard Clairvaux, "Jesus the Very Thought of Thee" (hymn).
⁶ Brown, *Galatians*, 208.
⁷ For the views on the nature of this ailment, see the various commentaries on Paul's Epistle to the Galatians.

We need to hear this. Paul's ailment was no impediment to the furtherance of the gospel among the Galatians. As a matter of fact, his weakness was what God used to magnify his power. That's an important lesson. As Thomas Schreiner notes, "The church advances as it proclaims a crucified Lord and lives a crucified life. The beauty of Christ is reflected in the humble and glad suffering of its messengers."[8] That runs contrary to everything we want to believe. We're drawn to beauty, we're enamored with money and success, and we're bewitched by power and prestige. Far too often, we think that these things are the weapons of our warfare. They aren't. God is most glorified when we are weakest. How do we view our illness, inability, depression, or any other form of weakness? We must learn to embrace these weaknesses as a means by which God delights to demonstrate his power.

A question
"What then has become of your blessedness? For I testify to you that, if possible, you would have gouged out your eyes and given them to me. Have I then become your enemy by telling you the truth?" (4:15–16). Paul's message of reconciliation was the cause of their "blessedness." At one time, they grasped this to such a degree that they were willing to have "gouged out" their eyes for him. This is likely a case of hyperbole. Paul is reminding the Galatians that they were ready to suffer for him. In sharp contrast, they're now questioning his apostolic authority; moreover, they're questioning his message. One day they're ready to suffer for him, but the next day they view him as an "enemy." What has happened? Paul has become their "enemy" by simply telling them the truth, and yet he persists in extending God's grace to them.

We need to hear this. We must never lose sight of the relationship between truth and grace. They're inseparable companions. Truth cuts, but grace heals. Truth stings, but grace soothes. Truth disturbs, but grace comforts. Truth demands that we declare what a righteous God says. With all earnestness, we seek to convey what he thinks about sin. However, grace demands that we declare what a compassionate God says. While we declare his utter displeasure with sin and sinners, we do so against the backdrop of his abounding mercy. Where there's brokenness for sin, he promises healing. Where there's conviction for sin, he promises mercy. Where there's weari-

---

[8] Schreiner, *Galatians*, 291.

ness for sin, he promises rest. Where there's repentance for sin, he promises forgiveness. Grace always proclaims what God says, in the shadow of the cross.

A comparison
"They make much of you, but for no good purpose. They want to shut you out, that you may make much of them. It is always good to be made much of for a good purpose, and not only when I am present with you, my little children, for whom I am again in the anguish of childbirth until Christ is formed in you!" (4:17-19). The false teachers are self-serving; as a result, they attempt to isolate the Galatians from Paul. He's in anguish on account of their spiritual condition. He labours for one reason—that Christ might be "formed" in them. This is the longing of his heart—conformity to Christ. (1) Conformed to his suffering—willing to suffer humbly, willingly, and joyfully. (2) Conformed to his death—willing to die to sin and temptation. (3) Conformed to his life—willing to submit all of life to the Word. (4) Conformed to his character—willing to put on the mind of Christ: compassion, kindness, humility, meekness, and patience.

We need to hear this. The birth of a child is a beautiful moment, but what precedes the birth isn't so beautiful. There's anguish. Paul draws a comparison between the anguish of giving birth and the anguish of engaging in ministry. "I am again in the anguish of childbirth until Christ is formed in you" (4:19). There's a cost to ministry. It's difficult. Faithful ministry means sleepless nights and anxious moments. But the cost is tinged with joy—the prospect of seeing men and women conformed to Christ. As John declares, "I have no greater joy than to hear that my children are walking in the truth" (3 John 1:4).

Conclusion
Paul ends this section as follows: "I wish I could be present with you now and change my tone, for I am perplexed about you" (4:20).[9] He's troubled by what's happening in the churches of Galatia. Error has supplanted truth, and consequently they're in danger of forsaking the gospel. His concern for their spiritual well-being is so great that he wishes he could be present with them. He wants them to know that he isn't about to abandon them without a fight.

---

[9] See 1:6, 9; 3:1; 5:12.

He's determined to challenge the legalism that has spread among them by pointing them to the sole sufficiency of Christ.

This struggle isn't unique to Paul's day. We're all legalists by nature. Deeply entrenched in our fallen nature is the conviction that there's something in us that explains why God loves us, forgives us, and welcomes us. We think like this because we're riddled with pride. "Self-love makes us conceive the best things about ourselves," warns William Perkins.[10] But the gospel tells us that we're without any merit in God's sight. It makes everything of God's grace and nothing of man's merit. It proclaims that God loves freely, forgives freely, and welcomes freely in Christ. Do we believe this? "Thanks be to God for his inexpressible gift!" (2 Cor. 9:15).

---

[10] Perkins, *Galatians*, 2:286.

15
Two Sons (4:21-31)

Let's imagine you're a Gentile, living in Galatia in the first century. Your city is full of idols, shrines, and temples. You lead your family in worshiping your household gods. You join the other tradesmen in your guild to conduct business while sacrificing to your patron god. You gather in the city centre with your fellow citizens to participate in festivals in honour of the gods. You know of some Jews who don't engage in these things. They have their own religion: they read a holy book (the Torah) and follow their own peculiar rules and rituals. One day, a man (named Paul) visits your city. He preaches in the local synagogue and market square. There's nothing particularly noteworthy about him. He isn't very charismatic, nor is he trained in rhetoric. To make matters worse, he's clearly unwell. Out of curiosity, you go to hear him. He claims that God has made him "a light to the Gentiles, that [he] may bring salvation to the ends of the earth" (Acts 13:47). He tells you about your sin, and he warns of God's coming judgment. He explains how Christ bore God's judgment on behalf of sinners. He talks about a coming resurrection. He announces that God forgives those who believe in Christ. You're convicted of your sin, and you believe in Christ. You turn from sin and idolatry to worship God. You're baptized. What a season of blessing! Many of your neighbours believe in Christ. Paul organizes all of you into what he calls a church.

After a short time, Paul leaves to preach the gospel in another city. Several months pass. One Sunday morning, you gather with your fellow believers to worship. There are some visitors present in the meeting. They're Jews. That isn't surprising, since many of the first converts were Jews. What is surprising is that they won't eat with you because they say you're unclean. You object: "That isn't what Paul taught us." But these men inform you (and everyone else) that you've been misled. Apparently, Paul isn't a real apostle, and he doesn't preach the full gospel. They inform you that God made a covenant with Abraham, and that only the physical descendants of Abraham's son (Isaac) are the beneficiaries of this covenant. They explain that God made another covenant with Moses, and that it's binding for all God's people. It shows how they're to live and how they're to acquire eternal life. They tell you that, in addition to believing in Christ, you must live under the law. For starters, you must be circumcised. Until you are, they can't have anything to do with you. You're beginning to wonder if there might be something to what they're saying. After all, they're Jews. The discussion goes on for some time. Some of the members of the church conform to the requirements of the law, but you're still on the fence. Then, to everyone's surprise, a letter arrives from Paul.

In his letter Paul speaks directly to those who "desire to be under the law" (4:21)—that is, those who believe they must keep the OT law to be saved. He presents four main arguments to show them the folly of their thinking.

An Argument from Experience (3:1-5)
"Did you receive the Spirit by works of the law or by hearing with faith?" (3:3)

An Argument from Scripture (3:6-4:7)
"Is the law then contrary to the promise of God?" (3:21)

An Argument from Experience (4:8-20)
"What then has become of the blessing you felt?" (4:15)

An Argument from Scripture (4:21-31)
"Do you not listen to the law?" (4:21)

An Appeal (5:1-12)

In his fourth argument, Paul contends that those "who desire to be under the law" (the Mosaic covenant) don't really listen to the law (the Torah) (4:21). To prove it, he appeals to a well-known historical event recorded in Genesis 16 and 21.

Illustration (4:22-26)

Abraham had "two sons" (4:22). Paul doesn't name them because everyone knows who they are: Ishmael and Isaac. Ishmael was born of "a slave woman" (Hagar), whereas Isaac was born of "a free woman" (Sarah) (4:22).[1] In

---

[1] See Romans 4:19.

addition, Ishmael was born "according to the flesh" (human effort), whereas Isaac was born "through promise" (divine grace) (4:23).

Paul declares that these historical events may be "interpreted allegorically" (4:24). How so? The two women are two covenants (4:24). Hagar is Mount Sinai, and her children are slaves (4:25). She represents the "present Jerusalem"—all those who believe that salvation rests on human effort (i.e., keeping the old covenant). Sarah is Mount Zion, and her children are free (4:26). She represents "the Jerusalem above"—all those who believe that salvation rests on divine grace.

Quotation (4:27)

Paul proceeds to quote Isaiah 54:1, "Rejoice, O barren one who does not bear; break forth and cry aloud, you who are not in labor! For the children of the desolate one will be more than those of the one who has a husband." The context is Israel's return from exile in Babylon. Israel is like a barren woman whose children have been lost, but God promises to retore her to the land where she will multiply. Paul's point is that the restoration from exile has arrived in the gospel—the salvation of Jews and Gentiles in Christ.

Application (4:28-31)

Paul wants to make sure his audience gets his point. And so, he applies his illustration as follows. (1) Believing Gentiles are "like Isaac" (4:28, 31). This means they're "children of the promise." Their mother is Sarah, and they're free. (2) Unbelieving Jews are like Ishmael (4:28, 31). This means they're children of "the flesh." Their mother is Hagar, and they're enslaved. (3) Just like Ishmael persecuted Isaac, so too unbelieving Jews persecute believing Gentiles (4:29).

At this point, Paul quotes Genesis 21:10, "Cast out the slave woman and her son" (4:30). He's aware that the Jews interpret this statement as meaning that God has rejected the Gentiles. They use it to justify their hatred of the Gentiles. In the immediate context, they appeal to it to defend their argument that if Gentiles (who believe in Christ) really want to be saved, then they better become Jews—that is, live under the OT law. But, according to Paul, who's the slave woman (Hagar) and her son (Ishmael)? The unbelieving Jews! Therefore, who's cast out? The unbelieving Jews!

Conclusion

Over the years, I've met a few Torah-observing Gentiles. They keep kosher and observe the Sabbath. They celebrate Passover and Sukkot (the Feast of Booths), but not Christmas or Easter. They learn some Hebrew and travel as much as possible to Israel. They use the word "Hashem" ("the name") when speaking of God. They believe that Jesus is the Messiah but refer to him as *Yeshua*. They post mezuzahs (little parchments of Deuteronomy 6:4-6) on their doors. Their central belief is that the NT is an extension of the Torah and, therefore, the Torah is still binding. In sum, they want to observe the Torah in the way they think *Yeshua* did.

Paul's admonition speaks directly to them: "Tell me, you who desire to be under the law, do you not listen to the law?" (4:21). Do you not understand that God gave a promise to Abraham (3:16)? He then established a temporary covenant with Moses to prepare for the fulfillment of his promise (3:17). Do you not understand that "when the fullness of time had come, God sent forth his son" (4:4)? He was "born under the law to redeem those who were under the law." All that to say, the law has passed away because Christ has fulfilled it. Christ is the realization of God's promise to Abraham. Do you not understand that all who believe in Christ are "children of promise" (4:28)? They're children of the "free woman" (4:31). Why would anyone "desire to be under the law"?

While we might not have any desire "to be under the law" as a means of salvation, we aren't immune to the impulse that gives rise to such a desire. I'm referring, of course, to our proclivity to legalism—the nagging notion that "the flesh" (human effort) is a contributing factor in our salvation. Given this perpetual struggle, here's a question we must always keep before us: Are we resting in God's grace?

Paul proclaims, "For God has done what the law, weakened by the flesh, could not do. By sending his own Son in the likeness of sinful flesh and for sin, he condemned sin in the flesh, in order that the righteous requirement of the law might be fulfilled in us, who walk not according to the flesh but according to the Spirit" (Rom. 8:3-4). What exactly did God do?

First, God sent his Son "in the likeness of sinful flesh and for sin."[2] In other words, Christ's death was a substitutionary sacrifice. By his death, he satisfied God's justice, thereby securing God's mercy on behalf of sinners.

---

[2] God sent his Son "for sin"; that is, "as an offering for sin." See Leviticus 4:3, Numbers 8:8, Psalm 39:6, Hebrews 10:6.

Second, God "condemned sin in the flesh." This means God imputed sin to Christ and punished him accordingly. He did this "so that the righteous requirement of the law might be fulfilled in us." The law requires righteousness from us, but it can't produce what it requires. Why? "It was weakened by the flesh"—that is, sinful human nature. As a result of our sin, therefore, we're condemned. However, Christ has taken that condemnation upon himself; furthermore, he has fulfilled the righteousness of the law. And so, when we're united to him by faith, the penalty is removed, and his righteousness is imputed to us. In this way, then, he has canceled "the record of debt that stood against us" (Col. 2:14). Infinite justice was satisfied, and infinite mercy was secured, at the cross. We're enriched by Christ's poverty, filled by his emptiness, exalted by his disgrace, healed by his wounds, comforted by his pain, and justified by his condemnation.

> Because the sinless Saviour died,
> our sinful soul is counted free.
> Because God the just is satisfied,
> to look on Christ and pardon me.[3]

Are we resting in Christ's sole sufficiency? When God justifies sinners, he imputes Christ's righteousness to them; hence, they stand before him, clothed in Christ's righteousness. To rest in Christ is to remember that we are one with him. What is ours is his—sin. What is his is ours—righteousness. The more we look to Christ, therefore, the stronger our faith will be.

> This will be found religion only, to bottom all our happiness upon the everlasting mountains of God's love and grace in Christ Jesus, to live continually in the sight of his infinite righteousness and merits. These are sanctifying sights, and without them the heart is carnal. You will then see the full vileness of sin, and yet see all pardoned; you will see your polluted self, and all your weak performances accepted through the mediation of the Holy Jesus; you will trample upon all your own works, self-glories, righteousness, and privileges, as of no value, and will be continually admiring the righteousness of Christ alone; yea you

---

[3] Charitie L. Bancroft, "Before the Throne of God Above" (hymn).

will rejoice in the ruin of all your own excellencies, that the Lord Jesus alone as Mediator may be exalted upon his throne of mercy.[4]

---

[4] Thomas Wilcox, *A Guide to Eternal Glory; or, Brief Directions to all Christians how to attain to Everlasting Life* (London, 1699), 20.

16
The Offense of the Cross (5:1-12)

There's a woman locked in a mere form of godliness. She's always in place on Sunday morning. She reads her Bible and prays every day. Her orthodoxy is stellar. She can sniff out a heretic a mile away. She's happy when the preacher tells the truth but feels he should leave the application to the Holy Spirit. She likes it when the preacher addresses hypocrisy, and she sincerely hopes Mrs. Jones was listening. She lives life in the accusative case. She's very quick to let people know when they haven't reached the required standard. Listening to her is like drinking vinegar. Then, one day, she begins to feel her heart-sins. She weeps over them. She forgets about all her grievances. She's enraptured with the glory of God. She's found talking with others about the beauty of Christ. She's filled with thankfulness. Her prayers become the stutters of a broken heart. Her prayers crash like waves upon the shores of heaven.[1]

What has happened? The Holy Spirit has freed this woman from the grip of legalism. Without a doubt, legalism is the default position of the human heart. The legalist rejects the doctrine of radical depravity—not necessarily in confession, but certainly in practice. The legalist doesn't think his sin is as serious as the Bible portrays it because he defines sin according to external actions rather than internal desires. The legalist creates a list of identifiable markers and convinces himself that his adherence to this list constitutes obedience thereby securing God's favour.

Legalism deceives. It may exist in practice even when grace is preached in theory. It's easy to proclaim the primacy of grace yet still live as though human effort is the determining factor in salvation.

Legalism diverts. It draws attention away from things that really enslave us. It obsesses over externals while never uttering a word about pride, envy, gossip, greed, covetousness, or gluttony. In short, it diverts attention away from sins of the heart.

---

[1] Jeremy Walker, *source unknown.*

Legalism destroys. Its poison spreads throughout the soul, blinding the eyes and plugging the ears. It fractures the joy of friendship and fellowship. It deadens the heart, leaving but a hollow shell.

The churches of Galatia are struggling with legalism. What is the main point of contention? Some people insist that it's necessary to "be under the law" to be saved (4:21).[2] By so doing, they're undermining the sole sufficiency of Christ (1:6-7). The Galatian believers are in danger of falling away. Out of deep pastoral concern, Paul seeks to dismantle this false teaching by way of four main arguments:

An Argument from Experience (3:1-5)
"Did you receive the Spirit by works of the law or by hearing with faith?" (3:3)

An Argument from Scripture (3:6-4:7)
"Is the law then contrary to the promise of God?" (3:21)

An Argument from Experience (4:8-20)
"What then has become of the blessing you felt?" (4:15)

An Argument from Scripture (4:21-31)
"Do you not listen to the law?" (4:21)

Paul follows up these arguments with an earnest appeal: "For freedom Christ has set us free; stand firm therefore, and do not submit again to a yoke of slavery" (5:1). Paul has already stated that Christ sets us "free" from slavery to sin (1:5) and slavery to the curse (3:13), but these aren't what he has in mind in 5:1. The "yoke of slavery" refers to the Jews' standing under the old covenant. Paul's point is that Christ has fulfilled the requirements of the old covenant and established a new covenant. Some in the churches of Galatia deny this, and insist that all must "be under the law." For Paul, this is to "submit again to a yoke of slavery."

---

[2] Thomas Schreiner summarizes the Jews' misunderstanding of the nature of God's righteousness as follows: "They did not subject themselves to God's saving gift of righteousness because they were ignorant that righteousness is a divine gift. This ignorance led them to the vain pursuit of trying to establish their own righteousness—a righteousness based on 'doing' (Romans 9:32; 10:5) instead of believing (Romans 9:32-33; 10:6-13). Here Paul counters a form of works-righteousness by which the Jews thought they could attain right standing with God." *The Law and Its Fulfillment: A Pauline Theology of Law* (Grand Rapids: Baker Books, 2001), 134.

The Offense of the Cross (5:1-12)

To submit to this yoke is to be severed from Christ (5:2-4)

Paul makes it clear that if the Galatians "accept circumcision" (that is, choose to live under the OT law), then they're "obligated" to keep the whole law (5:2-3). After all, if obedience of one point is required, then obedience of every point is required. The implication is obvious: "You are severed from Christ, you who would be justified by the law; you have fallen away from grace" (5:4).

Christ gave himself for our sins to deliver us from the present evil age (1:4). He was born under the law to redeem those who were under the law (4:5). He has secured God's forgiveness by means of his atoning work. Since he has done so, there's no longer any provision for the forgiveness of sins under the OT law. Therefore, those who choose to put themselves under the law are on their own. In a word, they're "severed from Christ."

To submit to this yoke is to fall away from grace (5:4-6)

Christ alone is the *grounds* of our justification, and faith alone is the *means* of our justification. Paul's contention is that those who seek to be justified by the OT law have denied both the grounds and means of justification and, therefore, they "have fallen from grace" (5:4). They've fallen from what they *profess*, not what they *possess*, for nothing can separate us from God's love in Christ (Rom. 8:39). Paul doesn't deny this reality in 5:4, but emphasizes that those who "desire to be under the law" reject the only way to be justified, which is by grace.

In marked contrast to these legalists, believers "eagerly wait for the hope of righteousness" (5:5). As Schreiner explains, "The eschatological hope of believers is the final declaration of righteousness on the last day. In the interim believers wait for that end-time declaration in reliance on the Holy Spirit and place their trust in Christ."[3] The gospel isn't about what we do, but what Christ has done. The only thing that "counts," therefore, is "faith working through love" (5:6). This means that faith is always dynamic. Elsewhere, Paul writes, "The aim of our charge is love that issues from a pure heart and a good conscience and a sincere faith" (1 Tim. 1:5). Faith is the *cause* of love while love is the *fruit* of faith. Logically, a cause (faith) does not receive any efficacy from its effect (love). Love is simply the operation of faith. "Faith and love are two hands of our soul," writes William Perkins. "Faith is a hand

---

[3] Schreiner, *Galatians*, 315.

that lays hold of Christ, and it does (as it were) pull him and his benefits into our souls. But love is a hand of another kind, for it serves not to receive in, but to give out the good it has and to communicate itself unto others."[4]

Faith is the instrument by which we become one with Christ. Because we're united to the One who is life, we come to life. The main indicator of spiritual life is love for God, his glory, his people, and his Word. We're so overwhelmed by the magnitude of God's forgiveness, we lose sight of ourselves in loving others.

To submit to this yoke is to disobey the truth (5:7–12)

Paul says that the Galatian believers were "running well," but someone "hindered" them from "obeying the truth" (5:7). The verb "hinder" literally means to "cut in" on another runner thereby causing him to stumble. The false teachers' insistence that salvation comes by way of observing the OT law is troubling the Galatians (1:7). It's hindering them from trusting in Christ alone. For Paul, this teaching isn't from God (5:8). Furthermore, it spreads like "leaven" and brings a "penalty" (5:9–10).

The false teachers, says Paul, are motivated by their desire to avoid "the offense of the cross" (5:11). When we preach the cross, we're saying that man is so radically depraved that God won't accept anything from him. This is offensive to the natural man because it refuses to allow him to establish righteousness based on his effort or ability. It's the main reason the Jews persecute Paul, and the main reason they insist that observance of the OT law is required for salvation. "Circumcision," explains Schreiner, "nullifies the scandal of the cross because it establishes righteousness based on human ability."[5]

The Jews look to their religious obedience (Rom. 2:17–24) and religious observance (Rom. 2:25–29) as the reason God favours them. They convince themselves that they're "a guide to the blind," "a light to those who are in darkness," "a corrector of the foolish," "a teacher of the children" (Rom. 2:19–20). In other words, they see themselves as superior to the Gentiles. Because they refuse to see themselves as they really are, they boast in the works of the law (Rom. 3:27). The term "boasting" comes from the battlefield. Goliath, for example, boasted before the armies of Israel (1 Sam. 17:8–11). These enemies of the gospel want to "boast" before God. But Paul says,

---

[4] Perkins, *Galatians*, 2:332–334.
[5] Schreiner, *Galatians*, 327.

"We hold that one is justified by faith apart from works of the law" (Rom. 3:28). This is what makes the gospel such a "stumbling block" to the Jews (1 Cor. 1:23). They resent the implication that their observance of the OT law is of no merit in God's sight, and they resent any suggestion that their standing before God is no different than that of the Gentiles.

This false teaching is so serious that Paul declares, "I wish those who unsettle you would emasculate themselves!" (5:12). He isn't expressing his desire for personal revenge, but his concern over the threat this false teaching poses to God's people. The false teachers distort the gospel (1:7). Paul knows that to err here is to err for all eternity, and so he pronounces a curse upon them. If the Galatian believers continue down this road, they too will be cursed. What we believe matters, especially when it has direct bearing on the gospel. We can't divide salvation between Christ's work and our work. He contributes everything, while we contribute nothing. Christ's merit is sufficient, and his mercy is abundant. "For in Christ Jesus neither circumcision nor uncircumcision counts for anything, but only faith working through love" (5:6).

Conclusion

We're free in Christ—free from the devil, the curse, and the law. We must "stand firm" and not "submit" to any form of slavery, namely, any suggestion that we can earn God's favour by means of "the flesh" (human effort). In Luke 18:10-13, Christ introduces us to the Publican and Pharisee. The first is conscious of his sin, and declares, "God, be merciful to me, a sinner!" The second is blind to his sin and proclaims, "God, I thank you that I am not like other men, extortioners, unjust, adulterers, or even like this tax collector." John Bunyan describes the Publican and Pharisee as "two men in whose condition the whole world is comprehended.[6] In other words, there are only two kinds of people in this world: those who know they're sinners and those who don't.

The gospel really is an apparent paradox. On the one hand, it drives us from God, in that it shows us our sin; it shows us our hopelessness and helplessness; it shows us that we're condemned in God's sight. On the other hand, it drives us to God. Recognizing our utter inability to do anything to please God, we run to him alone for mercy. The doctrine of justification ex-

---

[6] John Bunyan, *A Discourse upon the Pharisee and the Publican*, in *The Miscellaneous Works of John Bunyan*, ed. Owen Watkins (Oxford: Clarendon Press, 1988), 10:111.

cludes all boasting because it means we receive everything from God, and we humbly confess our complete dependence upon his mercy.

Section 4:
The Gospel "Applied" (5:13–6:10)

17
Called to Freedom (5:13-15)

We've been following a very simple outline as we've made our way through Paul's Epistle to the Galatians.

Salutation (1:1-5)
Caution (1:6-10)

Paul defends the authority of his mission:
    (1) The Gospel "Revealed" (1:11-2:14)
    (2) The Gospel "Explained" (2:15-21)

Paul defends the accuracy of his message:
    (3) The Gospel "Defended" (3:1-5:12)
    (4) The Gospel "Applied" (5:13-6:10)

Caution (6:11-17)
Benediction (6:18)

Having considered the first three sections, we now come to the fourth: the Gospel Applied (5:13-16:10). Back in 5:1, Paul addresses the threat of *legalism*: "For freedom Christ has set us free; stand firm therefore, and do not submit again to a yoke of slavery." Some are teaching that it's necessary to be "under" the OT law, to obtain a right standing before God. Paul challenges this idea by affirming that Christ frees us from the obligation to fulfill the law. He has fulfilled it, and he has absorbed its curse. By faith in Christ, we become one with him and obtain a right standing before God. We're free in Christ.

Now, in 5:13, Paul addresses another threat, namely, *libertinism*: "For you were called to freedom, brothers. Only do not use your freedom as an opportunity for the flesh, but through love serve one another." Since the start of the letter, Paul has emphasized the believer's freedom in Christ. He knows his comments are open to misinterpretation. Some might conclude that we're free to live however we please.[1] Here's what Paul wants them (and us) to grasp: freedom isn't the liberty to do what we want, but the liberty to do what God wants.[2] As John Calvin notes, "We subject ourselves to God and allow our lives to be so governed by his will that things most bitter to us (because they come from him) become sweet to us."[3] This is precisely Paul's point in 5:13–15.

Freedom is denying the flesh (5:13)

"For you were called to freedom, brothers. Only do not use your freedom as an opportunity for the flesh."

The "flesh" refers to our propensity to self-love, which alienates us from God. It enslaves us, darkening our minds, hardening our hearts, and binding our wills. It's death; it's at war with God; it's unable to obey God; it's unable to please God; and we're helpless to do anything about it (Rom. 8:6–8). For this reason, we must be born again (John 3:3). The new birth includes the enlightening of the darkened mind, the softening of the hardened heart, and the liberating of the enslaved will. It's a new condition, which gives rise to a new inclination.

The reality is, however, that we're only renewed in part. After the new birth, the flesh remains. There are now two semi-intact motivational systems within us: the flesh (love of self) and the Spirit (love of God). They wage war against one another. Paul's point is that, by God's grace, we possess the freedom to deny the flesh. The dominion of sin has been broken and, therefore, we're no longer enslaved to it (Rom. 6:6).

Freedom is serving the church (5:13)

"For you were called to freedom, brothers. ... through love serve one another."

Because freedom in Christ liberates us from the desires of the flesh (i.e., selfishness), we now serve one another. "Faith deals with invisibles," says Thomas Watson, "but God hates that love which is invisible."[4] Such loving service is characterized by affection, tenderness, sacrifice, giving, and forgiveness. We no longer think in terms of what we want, desire, or deserve;

---

[1] See Romans 6:1–23.
[2] See 1 Peter 2:16.
[3] John Calvin, as quoted in Donald K. McKim, *The Cambridge Companion to John Calvin* (Cambridge University Press, 2004), 148.
[4] Quoted in Thomas, *A Puritan Golden Treasury*, 174.

Called to Freedom (5:13-15)

rather, we think of others ahead of ourselves. "Let each of us please his neighbour for his good, to build them up" (Rom. 15:2). When the gospel takes hold, we pursue what makes for peace and edification in the church, and we serve one another through love.

> May the mind of Christ, my Saviour,
> live in me from day to day;
> By his love and power controlling
> all I do and say.
>
> May the love of Jesus fill me
> as the waters fill the sea;
> Him exalting, self-abasing,
> O this is victory.[5]

Freedom is fulfilling the law (5:14)

"For you were called to freedom, brothers. ... For the whole law is fulfilled in one word: 'You shall love your neighbor as yourself.'"

When the law is viewed as a ladder to heaven (a righteousness of works), then it stands in an antithetical relationship to the gospel (a righteousness of grace). But we must never allow this antithetical relationship to detract from a positive view of the law, especially those parts of it which are an expression of God's eternal will. We refer to these as his "moral" law. It corresponds to that which is written on man's heart by nature (Rom. 2:15). It wasn't given as a reaction to man's fall or as a mere component of Israel's religion. On the contrary, it's permanent in the plan of God. According to John Calvin, it's useful to believers in that it gives a clearer understanding of God's will for their lives, and it continues to convict thereby cultivating a sense of need within them.[6]

Contrary to popular misconception, this use of the moral law isn't legalism. In the New Covenant, Jeremiah speaks of God putting his law within his people (Jer. 31:31-33) whereas Ezekiel speaks of God putting his Spirit within them (Ezek. 36:26-27). An appreciation of the relationship between the law and the Spirit is pivotal. Because we're born of the Spirit, we love God with all our heart, soul, and mind, thereby fulfilling the law.[7] As believers, we have

---

[5] Kate B. Wilkinson, "May the Mind of Christ, My Saviour" (hymn).
[6] Calvin, *Institutes*, 2:12.
[7] See Leviticus 19:18; Deuteronomy 6:3-5; 10:12-13; Matthew 22:37-40; Romans 10:13.

the Holy Spirit within us, and he writes the law upon our hearts. This means that he causes us to love God. Because we love God, we want to know his will and do his will, and we find his will expressed in his moral law. Obedience, therefore, isn't an attempt to obtain a meritorious standing before God; rather, it's the fruit of our love for God.

This is confirmed in Romans 13:9, where Paul quotes four of the Ten Commandments (Exod. 20:13-17). His point is that loving our neighbour means we're committed to our neighbour's well-being. "Love does no wrong to a neighbor" (Rom. 13:10). We love our neighbour by not committing adultery (Exod. 20:14), not murdering (Exod. 20:13), not stealing (Exod. 20:15), and not coveting (Exod. 20:17). In short, we love our neighbour by pursuing for him what we want for ourselves. Do we want respect? We should respect others. Do we want help? We should help others. Do we want compassion? We should show compassion toward others. Are we lonely? We should befriend someone. Are we upset? We should comfort someone. Are we hungry? We should feed someone. This is the fulfillment of the law, and this is freedom in Christ.

Freedom is keeping the peace (5:15)

"For you were called to freedom, brothers. ... But if you bite and devour one another, watch out that you are not consumed by one another."

Whenever and wherever there's "biting" and "devouring" (i.e., people going at each other like wild animals), we know the flesh (self-love) reigns. In this case, the issue isn't what we believe, but how we hold what we believe. The issue is how we communicate with others, how we view others, and how we treat others.

In contrast, whenever and wherever there's peace, we know that people are enjoying their freedom in Christ. Despite differences, disagreements, and disappointments, there's still love for one another and devotion to one another. Those who aren't free in Christ are discontent, unhappy, resentful, proud, judgmental, and agitated, and they sow the seeds of discord wherever they go. But those who are free in Christ abound in his mercy. When they constitute a local church, they're a family characterized by compassion, kindness, humility, meekness, and patience (Col. 3:12). They "put on love, which binds everything together in perfect harmony" (Col. 3:14).

When we're free in Christ, we have the mechanism for overcoming our differences. The instinct to look down on other believers is one of the most obvious signs of a heart from which legalism has not been fully banished. It implies that we've merited the grace of God more than others. But when the gospel occupies the centre, we pursue what makes for peace and edification in the church (Rom. 14:19).

When we're free in Christ, we have the impetus for offering forgiveness and seeking reconciliation. When we contemplate the cross, we're crushed to the ground. We're overwhelmed by God's love for us, and we're compelled to extend compassion to others—even those who have mistreated us. We're willing to forgive "one another, as God in Christ forgave [us]" (Eph. 4:32). This is the starting point for healing strained relationships, broken marriages, shattered homes, and fractured churches.

When we're free in Christ, we have the solution for one of the most common sins among us. I'm referring to the sin of entitlement. We live in a bizarre age, in which we view ourselves as the protagonist in our life narrative. Because of our sense of entitlement, we think everyone must bend to our personal narrative. Only the gospel will uproot this sin. It does so by placing Christ alone at the centre of our lives. As a result, we're willing to surrender our rights because we have something of far greater significance in view. "The reproaches of those who reproached you fell on me" (Ps. 69:9). Christ was willing to endure underserved suffering, and he was willing to deny himself for the good of others. When he stands at the centre of our lives, he cultivates this same attitude in us.

Conclusion

According to William Hendriksen,

> The Christian religion resembles a narrow bridge over a place where two polluted streams meet: one is called legalism, the other libertinism. The believer must not lose his balance, lest he tumble into the refined faults of Judaism on the one side, or into the gross vices of paganism on the other. He must tread the safe and narrow path. Whether fashionable or course, both kinds of evils are products of "the flesh," that is, of sinful human nature.[8]

The legalist believes, "I can obey without knowing God's grace." The libertine believes, "I can know God's grace without obeying." Both are "pol-

---

[8] William Hendriksen, *New Testament Commentary: Exposition of Galatians* (Grand Rapids: Baker Books, 2007), 209.

luted streams" and perilous to the Christian life. Thankfully, in Galatians 5, Paul shows the absurdity of both. He shows us how to navigate the "narrow bridge." We do so by staying focused on two glorious truths: we're "free" in Christ (5:1), and we're free "through love to serve one another" (5:13).

18
Walking by the Spirit (5:16–17)

The Bible is emphatic: God requires righteousness of all who would enter his presence. Here's the bad news: we aren't righteous. Here's the good news: the righteousness God requires isn't found in us but in Christ who lived and died as our Mediator. As Paul indicates throughout his Epistle to the Galatians, Christ's righteousness is made ours by grace through faith in him. Paul also insists that the faith that unites us to Christ works "through love" (5:6). Self-love is transformed into selfless love because we're in vital union with Christ whose character the Holy Spirit now produces in us.

For Paul, this means that we must walk by the Spirit. He writes, "But I say, walk by the Spirit, and you will not gratify the desires of the flesh. For the desires of the flesh are against the Spirit, and the desires of the Spirit are against the flesh, for these are opposed to each other, to keep you from doing the things you want to do" (5:16–17). To grasp what Paul is saying, we must take careful note of four realities.[1]

There's a sin-desiring principle called "the flesh"
In the Garden, Adam's chief good and last end was God, but Adam rebelled and succumbed to the devil's temptation: "You will be like God" (Gen. 3:5). "When man fell from God, he fell to himself," writes Thomas Manton.[2] The result was "the flesh"—fallen human nature oriented towards self-love, self-autonomy, self-sufficiency, and self-gratification. This is now man's default position.

Christ declares, "What comes out of a person is what defiles him. For from within, out of the heart of man, come evil thoughts, sexual immorality, theft, murder, adultery, coveting, wickedness, deceit, sensuality, envy, slander, pride, foolishness. All these evil things come from within, and they defile a person" (Mark 7:21–23). In other words, our problem is not

---

[1] I am indebted to Manton for his insights in *Works*, 2:285–292.
[2] Manton, *Works*, 3:50.

external, but internal. Our problem resides in our corrupt heart. George Swinnock describes this predicament as follows:

> Original sin has debauched the mind, and made it think crooked things straight, and straight things crooked; loathsome things lovely, and lovely things loathsome. It has perverted the will, and made it, as a diseased stomach, to eat unwholesome food against reason. It has enthralled the affections to sensuality and brutishness. It has chained the whole man and delivered it up to the law of sin.[3]

The "affections" are the soul's dispositional drives—its inclination or disinclination to any given object. Prior to the fall, Adam's love was set on God and, consequently, his affections (desire delight, hate, fear, and sorrow) were well-directed; that is to say, they functioned properly. When Adam sinned, however, the object of his love changed. In his fallen condition, his love was no longer set on God, but *self*. As a result, his affections became "enthralled' (or disordered). And that has been the predicament of Adam's descendants ever since. We love what we should hate and hate what we should love.

Because of our "enthralled" affections, sin has dominion over us. Self-love corrupts our every thought, word, and deed. We're self-seeking rather than God-seeking (Rom. 2:6–8). This condition renders us helpless. To put it another way, we're so captivated by "the flesh" that we have no power to escape from it.

There's a God-desiring principle called "the Spirit"

God promises, "I will put my laws into their minds, and write them on their hearts" (Heb. 8:10). This is the new birth, whereby the Holy Spirit enlightens our mind so that we see God's will and inclines our heart so that we desire God's will. "They who are truly converted are new creatures," says Jonathan Edwards. "They have new hearts, new eyes, new ears, new tongues, new hands, and new feet. They walk in newness of life."[4]

The Holy Spirit change us by regeneration.[5] It is the restoration of God's image in us, whereby the faculties of the soul (mind, will, and affections) are renewed in knowledge, righteousness, and holiness (Eph. 4:24; Col. 3:10).

---

[3] Swinnock, *Works*, 2:166.
[4] Jonathan Edwards, *The Religious Affections* (Edinburgh: Banner of Truth, 1961), 313.
[5] See John 3:3; Ephesians 2:4–5; Colossians 2:13; Titus 3:4–6.

That is to say, the Holy Spirit illumines our darkened mind, liberates our enslaved will, and directs our disordered affections. In so doing, he renews our love for God.

The two principles (the Spirit and the flesh) oppose each other

The new birth is a new condition, which gives rise to a new inclination. But it's important to remember that we're only renewed in part. This means the flesh remains in the believer, and it's soon kindled. Therefore, the Spirit and the flesh (two principles) are mixed in us—in our minds, affections, and wills—and they oppose each other. They function as two semi-intact motivational systems within us: the "flesh" is love of self, whereas the "Spirit" is love of God. These two principles are diametrically opposed to each other. "The desires of the flesh are against the Spirit, and the desires of the Spirit are against the flesh, for these are opposed to each other, to keep you from doing the things you want to do" (5:17). Because of the flesh, we want to sin, but the Holy Spirit dwells within us; as a result, we're no longer free to do what the flesh desires but must follow the Holy Spirit's leading. "But I say, walk by the Spirit, and you will not gratify the desires of the flesh" (5:16).

When we walk by the Spirit, we subdue the desires of the flesh

We possess the freedom to say *no* to sin. "Though we are still weak," writes Thomas Manton, "yet we have the gift of the Spirit to free us from sin."[6] When we walk by the Spirit, the desires of the flesh are subdued. As the one principle grows, the other wanes. As the one principle strengthens, the other weakens. "Where the Spirit of the Lord is, there is freedom" (2 Cor. 3:17). J.I. Packer explains,

> God unites the individual to the risen Lord in such a way that the dispositional drives of Christ's perfect human character—the inner urgings, that is, to honour, adore, love, obey, serve and please God, and to benefit others for both their sake and his sake—are now reproduced at the motivational centre of that individual's being. And they are reproduced, in face of the contrary egocentric cravings of fallen nature, in a dominant way, so that the Christian, though still troubled and tormented by the urgings of indwelling sin, is no longer ruled by those urgings in the way that was true before. Being under grace, the Christian is freed from sin ... the motivational theocentricity of the heart set

---

[6] Manton, *Works*, 2:287.

free will prompt the actions that form the habits of Christ-likeness that constitute the Spirit's fruit (Gal. 5:22), and thus the holiness of radical repentance (daily abandonment of self-centred self-will), childlike humility (daily listening to what God says in his Word, and daily submission to what he sends in his providence), and love to God and humans that honours and serves both, will increasingly appear. This thoroughgoing intellectual and moral theocentricity, whereby Christians come to live no longer for themselves but for him who died and rose to save them (2 Cor. 5:15), is first God's gift and then the Christian's task, and as such it is the foundation not only of sounds ethics but also of true spirituality.[7]

Future glorification alone will mark the termination of our sin. For its part, regeneration ushers in a great conflict between the flesh (our love of self) and the Spirit (our love of God). That's why Paul writes, "So then, brothers, we are debtors, not to the flesh, to live according to the flesh. For if you live according to the flesh you will die, but if by the Spirit you put to death the deeds of the body, you will live" (Rom. 8:12-13). The verb, "put to death," is in the present tense, implying a continuous action. This is significant because it means that our killing of sin (i.e., love of self) is not a dramatic or climactic experience, but a continuous battle. To put it another way, it involves a daily weakening of sin at the motivational level.

John Owen observes two very important details concerning Paul's words in Romans 8:12-13.[8] The first is that mortification is the Holy Spirit's work: "by the Spirit." The second is that mortification is our work: "you put to death." At first glance, Paul seems to contradict himself. Is mortification the Holy Spirit's work or our work? The answer is both. As Owen explains:

> The Holy Spirit does not so work our mortification in us as not to keep it still an act of our obedience. The Holy Spirit works in us and upon us, as we are fit to be wrought in and upon; that is, so as to preserve our own liberty and free obedience. He works upon our understandings, wills, consciences, and affections, agreeably to their own natures. He works in us and with us, not against us or without us, so that his assistance is an encouragement as to the facilitating of the work, and no occasion of neglect as to the work itself.[9]

---

[7] J.I. Packer, *Serving the People of God*, in *The Collected Shorter Writings of J. I. Packer* (Carlisle: Paternoster, 2008), 2:259.

[8] Owen, *Works*, 6:5-16.

[9] Owen, *Works*, 6:20.

To put it another way, the Holy Spirit is the author of mortification in us because we mortify sin by his enabling grace and power. He alone is the agent of change because he alone is the source of quickening and enabling grace. "It is God who works in you, both to will and to work for his good pleasure" (Phil. 2:13). As the Spirit of light (Eph. 1:17), he gives us a sight and sense of our sin. As the Spirit of life (Rom. 8:2), he implants a new principle in us. As the Spirit of love (2 Tim. 1:7), he heightens our appreciation of God's love for us. We're the subordinate agent, meaning we subdue the flesh by God's grace. "His divine power has granted to us all things that pertain to life and godliness" (2 Peter 1:3).

Conclusion

Robert Murray M'Cheyne remarks, "Most of God's people are content to be saved from the hell that is without. They are not so anxious to be saved from the hell that is within. I fear there is little feeling of their need for the indwelling Spirit."[10] Is that true of you? Do you realize there's a hell within? As Paul indicates in 5:16-17, there's a sin-desiring principle called the flesh, and there's a God-desiring principle called the Spirit. These semi-intact motivational systems oppose each other. When we walk by the Spirit, we don't gratify the desires of the flesh.

In Texas, there are trees called "live" (or evergreen) oaks. Technically speaking, they aren't evergreens, but they're called evergreens because they keep their leaves throughout the winter. They begin to drop their leaves as new ones appear in the spring. Likewise, as we put on the new self, it pushes out the old self (Eph. 4:22-24). That's how we're "saved from the hell that is within."

---

[10] Robert Murray M'Cheyne, as quoted in Andrew Bonar, *Memoir and Remains of Robert Murray M'Cheyne* (Edinburgh: Oliphant, Anderson, and Ferrier, 1883), 198.

19
Keeping in Step with the Spirit (5:18-25)

Often, after a person is born again, and asks "What shall I do next?" he is given a list of things, usually of a limited nature, and primarily negative. Often, he is given the idea that if he does not do this series of things (whatever this series of things happens to be in the particular country and location and at the time he happens to live), he will be spiritual. This is not so ... we must still emphasize that the Christian life, or true spirituality, is more than refraining from a certain external list of taboos in a mechanical way.[1]

According to Paul, "faith working through love" shows itself in denying the flesh (5:13), serving the church (5:13), fulfilling the law (5:14), and keeping the peace (5:15). But how can we live like this? In a word, we must walk by the Spirit (5:16-17). This is the essence of "true spirituality."

Paul reiterates all this in 5:18-25, declaring, "But if you are led by the Spirit, you are not under the law" (5:18). The word "led" is used in reference to the blind man who cries out to Christ near Jericho. In response, Christ commands that the man be "led" to him (Luke 18:40). There's no point in telling the man where he should go, since he can't see anything. He must be "led" to Christ. Leading is more than simply pointing someone in the right direction. This is Paul's point in 5:18. By regeneration, the Holy Spirit imparts a new enabling which results in a life conformed to God's Word. "All true believers are being led by the Spirit," writes J.I. Packer. "It is that constant, effective, and beneficent influence which the Holy Spirit exercises within the hearts of God's children whereby they are being directed and enabled more and more to crush the power of indwelling sin and to walk in the way of God's commandments, freely and cheerfully."[2]

In his upper room discourse (John 14-17), Christ has a great deal to say about the Holy Spirit.[3] As the disciples gather, they're troubled (John 14:1),

---

[1] Francis A. Schaeffer, *True Spirituality* (Tyndale House Publishers, 1971), 4-5.
[2] Hendriksen, *Galatians*, 216-217.
[3] See John 14:16, 26; 15:26; 16:7.

but Christ encourages them: "I will ask the Father, and he will give you another Helper, to be with you forever, even the Spirit of truth" (John 14:16-17). A "helper" is someone who supports and strengthens someone else. The word "another" means of the same sort, implying that Christ is praying that the Father will send someone like him to be with his disciples. He adds, "It is to your advantage that I go away, for if I do not go away, the Helper will not come to you. But if I go, I will send him to you" (John 16:7).

Christ's promise is fulfilled in the baptism with the Holy Spirit. Paul declares, "For in one Spirit we were all baptized into one body" (1 Cor. 12:13). Christ is the agent by which this baptism occurs; the Holy Spirit is the element in which this baptism occurs; and identity in "one body" (the church) is the purpose for which this baptism occurs. Because we're baptized by Christ with the Holy Spirit into his body, we're now "led" by the Spirit. It's a positional reality. According to Paul, this means we aren't "under the law" (5:18). To be under the law is to be "under a curse" (3:10), "under sin" (3:22), "under a guardian" (3:25), "under guardians and managers" (4:2), and "under the elementary principles of the world" (4:3). But Christ was "born under the law" (4:4). In fulfilling its requirements, he redeems us—sets us free.

There's no power for change for those who are "under the law" because they're inclined to sin (self-love) and the law is powerless to do anything about it.[4] To be "under the law" is to be obligated to keep it and condemned for failing to do so. Thankfully, we've been set free from the law, and now we're "led" by the Spirit. What does this leading look like?

The Works of the Flesh (5:19–21)

To begin with, those who are "led" by the Spirit mortify the "works of the flesh." Paul leaves us in no doubt as to what these "works" (or vices) are, as he provides a detailed list. It's important to note the following.

First, the list isn't exhaustive. At the end of it, Paul adds these words, "and things like these" (5:21), thereby indicating that he has given but a sampling of "the works of the flesh."[5]

Second, the list is divided into four categories. Paul's aim is to show us how the "desires of the flesh" (5:17) impact us: (1) sexually—immorality

---

[4] See Romans 7:19–24.
[5] For other lists, see Matthew 25:41–46; Romans 1:29–32; 1 Corinthians 6:9–10; Ephesians 5:3–6; Revelation 22:12–16.

(unlawful intercourse), impurity (unnatural practices), and sensuality (uncontrolled desires); (2) religiously—idolatry and sorcery; (3) relationally—enmity, strife, jealousy, fits of anger, rivalries, dissensions, divisions, and envy; and (4) behaviourally—drunkenness and orgies (i.e., drinking orgies).

The third category (the relational) is the most pronounced of the four in the list. Why is that? It's likely that these particular "works of the flesh" were prevalent among the Galatian churches.

Fourth, "those who do such things will not inherit the kingdom of God." To indulge in any of these "works" is to declare that we aren't "led" by the Spirit. This kind of behaviour is so utterly inconsistent with what it means to be "in Christ" that, when people persist in it, there can be but one conclusion: they aren't believers. Paul's warning ought to terrify those who are flippant in their approach to sin.

The Fruit of the Spirit (5:22-23)

Secondly, those who are "led" by the Holy Spirit necessarily produce "the fruit of the Spirit." Observe the following:

First, the fruit is related to Christ-like character: love (John 15:17; Eph. 5:1-2); joy (Luke 10:21; John 15:11; Heb. 12:2); peace (John 14:27); patience (2 Peter 3:9, 15); kindness (Titus 2:11-12); goodness (Titus 3:4); faithfulness (Heb. 3:1-2); gentleness (Matt. 11:28-31; 12:20; 21:5); and self-control (Heb. 5:8; 1 Pet. 2:22-23). Interestingly, in his upper room discourse, Christ speaks about these things in relation to himself. He bids us abide in his "love" (John 15:9); he desires that his "joy" might remain in us (John 15:11); and he bestows his "peace" upon us (John 14:27). Of course, we see it throughout his ministry. We see it in his dealings with the sick, the young, the difficult, the discouraged, and the lost. He abounds in the fruit of the Spirit when the leper kneels before him, the men lower the paralytic at his feet, Jairus pleads with him to heal his daughter, and the woman with the hemorrhage touches his garment. We see it in his dealings with those who hate him. We see it when he prostrates himself to wash his disciples' feet. And we see it when he stretches out his arms upon Calvary's cross, and bears the sins of the world.

Second, there is only one fruit. The word is singular. It's impossible, therefore, to produce one grace without the others. It's impossible to be loving but not gentle. It's impossible to be kind but not faithful. The Holy Spirit produces this harmonious cluster of Christian graces in every believer.

Third, "against such things there is no law." By means of the fruit of the Spirit the works of the flesh are annihilated. In other words, the fruit of the Spirit pushes out the works of the flesh. This is something the law can never do.

Keeping in Step with the Spirit (5:24–25)

"And those who belong to Christ Jesus have crucified the flesh with its passions and desires" (5:24). Here Paul is thinking primarily of our union with Christ. Earlier, he declares, "I have been crucified with Christ. It is no longer I who live, but Christ who lives in me. And the life I now live in the flesh I live by faith in the Son of God, who loved me and have himself for me" (2:20). Upon the cross, Christ stood in my place. Because of my union with him through faith, his cross is made mine. Now I have communion with him in his life, death, and burial, meaning God imputes these to me as if I had performed them in my own person. I now see myself hanging on the cross. I no longer live for myself because I'm no longer identified with Adam (the old man) but with Christ (the new man). But I still live in a fallen world — "the present evil age" (1:4). The spiritual life, therefore, is one of tension. I live "by faith," meaning I submit to Christ "who loved me and gave himself for me."

Another way of saying this is as follows: "If we live by the Spirit, let us also walk with the Spirit" (5:25). In the original, the phrases "by the Spirit" and "with the Spirit" stand in the middle of the verse: "If we live by the Spirit, with the Spirit let us also walk." And so, what's Paul's point? He's emphasizing the difference between the indicative (we live by the Spirit) and the imperative (we must walk with the Spirit). That is to say: living by the Spirit is the root, while walking with the Spirit is the fruit.

Living by the Spirit

"If we live by the Spirit ..." The term "if" introduces a first-class conditional clause, which assumes that what follows is true. And so, we should understand Paul's statement as follows: "Since we live by the Spirit." In other words, he's stating a fact, not a possibility. As believers, we "live" by the Spirit; that is, we derive our life from him. It's his life (not the law) that makes us alive. God unites us to Christ by the Holy Spirit. As a result of this union, the Holy Spirit reproduces the perfect dispositional drives of Christ's human nature in us. We now possess new desires to love, obey, serve, and please God. This is evident in the fruit of the Spirit. While the flesh (love of self) still troubles us, it's no longer dominant.

Walking by the Spirit

"Let us also walk with the Spirit." The term "walk" (*stoichomen*) in 5:25 isn't the same term that's used for "walk" (*peripateo*) in 5:16. It literally means "to proceed in order." A better translation is "keep in step." Paul seems to be saying that, as we learned to walk physically by trial and error, we must learn to walk spiritually. We do so by focusing on what it means to belong to Christ: we've "crucified the flesh with its passions and desires" (5:24). This is our legal standing in him. Now, we're to behave as dead men in respect to the flesh. In effect, we hear God say to us: "Because you believe in Christ, by the Holy Spirit I have joined you to Christ. When he died, you died. When he rose, you rose. Now, act like it!" What does this mean for the "desires of the flesh" and "the works of the flesh"? John Stott tells us:

> If besetting sins persistently plague us, it is either because we have never truly repented, or because, having repented, we have not maintained our repentance. It is as if, having nailed our old nature to the cross, we keep wistfully returning to the scene of the execution. We begin to fondle it, to caress it, to long for its release, even to try to take it down again from the cross. We need to learn to leave it there. When some jealous, or proud, or malicious, or impure thought invades our mind we must kick it out at once. It is fatal to begin to examine it and consider whether we are going to give in to it or not. We have declared war on it; we are not going to resume negotiations. We have settled the issue for good; we are not going to reopen it. We have crucified the flesh; we are never going to draw the nails.[6]

Conclusion

God placed Adam in the Garden and commanded him to be fruitful and fill and subdue the earth (Gen. 1:28). But he failed and ushered in "the present evil age" (1:4), characterized by the "works of the flesh" (5:19). All these "works" arise from Adam's original sin. Mercifully, Christ has "delivered us from the present evil age" (1:4). He did so by fulfilling the law, suffering the

---

[6] Stott, *Galatians*, 151-152.

curse, and bearing the wrath of God. As a result, he has secured the promised gift of the Holy Spirit (1 Cor. 15:45).[7]

Throughout the time of his earthly humiliation, Christ himself was filled with the Holy Spirit. The Holy Spirit was the source of his ministerial gifts, and the source of his love, joy, peace, patience, kindness, goodness, faithfulness, gentleness, and self-control (5:22). Even now, during his present session at God's right hand, the Holy Spirit continues to fill Christ's human nature. And the Father sends the Holy Spirit through Christ into our lives, so that he produces in us the same fruit he produced in Christ. Those who are justified by grace alone through faith alone in Christ alone are empowered by the Holy Spirit to live in a new way.

---

[7] J. V. Fesko notes the relationship between the fruit of the Spirit and Isaiah's prophesy regarding the "shoot" that would come forth from the stump of Jesse. He would "bear fruit" as the Holy Spirit rests upon him (Isa. 11:1–5; 27:6). The language of "fruit" is symbolic for justice, righteousness, and peace (Isa. 32:14–17; 44:2–4; 45:8). The promised king, in turn, pours out the Holy Spirit upon his people so that they bear fruit. See Fesko, *Galatians*, 165–167.

20
The Fruit of the Spirit in Action: Avoiding Conceit (5:26)

Many years ago, I witnessed something I would like to forget—a face-slapping, eye-gouging, hair-pulling confrontation between two "Christian" women in the foyer of a church, where I happened to be preaching. A rare display of animosity? Thankfully, yes. A rare attitude of heart? Regrettably, no. The envy, bitterness, malice, and resentment, which gave rise to that unfortunate confrontation, is all too common among us. While far more subtle than any public "smack-down," it's just as damaging. It destroys relationships, divides churches, and dishonours Christ. At its root are the "desires" and "works" of the flesh (5:17, 19). It's for this reason that Paul, immediately following his command, "let us also walk with the Spirit" (5:25), issues another command: "Let us not become conceited, provoking one another, envying one another" (5:26).[1]

The Sin of Conceit
Conceit (or pride) is the sin of all sins. "It is," says Thomas Manton, "a lifting up of the heart above God and against God and without God."[2] Satan rebelled because he wanted to be like God. Adam and Eve rebelled because they wanted to be like God. Ever since the fall, man has been in love with *self*, and this is at the root of every sin. Because it's innate, it tarnishes our words, thoughts, and actions. I realize most people don't agree with this. According to the prevailing wisdom, our greatest need is self-esteem. This is a fallacy. No-one lacks self-esteem. Encouraging people to grow in their self-esteem is like adding gasoline to a brush fire to extinguish it. By nature, we're con-

---

[1] Paul has already spoken of "biting and devouring one another in 5:15. The attention he gives to this sin seems to indicate that it was prevalent among the churches of Galatia. Interestingly, he places jealousy, rivalries, divisions, and envy on the same level as idolatry, sorcery, and immorality (5:19-21). He makes it clear that those who practice "such things" won't inherit God's kingdom.

[2] Quoted in Thomas, *A Puritan Golden Treasury*, 223.

sumed with ourselves. "Everyone who is proud in heart is an abomination to the LORD" (Prov. 16:5).

Thankfully, Christ reconciles us to God through the blood of his cross. The problem is that peace with God leads to conflict with three enemies, namely, the devil, the world, and the flesh. Of these three Paul is particularly concerned about the flesh and the threat it poses to the believer: "The desires of the flesh are against the Spirit, and the desires of the Spirit are against the flesh, for these are opposed to each other" (5:17).[3] There's a battle raging between our love of self (the flesh) and our love of God (the Spirit). It rages on many fronts, but the most serious is this: Who will be uppermost?

We want people to think highly of us, and we want to be esteemed, admired, and praised. As William Gurnall warns, "Pride loves to climb up, not as Zacchaeus to see Christ, but to be seen."[4] This desire to be uppermost manifests itself in two main ways. (1) For some, it shows itself in a superiority complex. The most obvious signs of those who want to prove their superiority are impatience when frustrated and defensiveness when criticized. (2) For others, it manifests itself in an inferiority complex. The most obvious signs of those who want to disprove their inferiority are criticism of others and avoidance of others.

If we aren't embracing and applying the gospel, conceit will rule over our hearts. The result will be relational chaos: "enmity, strife, jealousy, fits of anger, rivalries, dissensions, divisions, envy" (5:20–21).

Envying One Another

Conceit leads to "envying one another"—what James calls "bitter jealousy" (Jas. 3:14). According to Jonathan Edwards, "[Envy] is a disposition natural in men, that they love to be uppermost; and this disposition is directly crossed, when they see others above them."[5] (1) It's *angry*. It's easily agitated and provoked; it's always finding fault with others; and it's always venting and criticizing. (2) It's *moody*. It's irritable and resentful; it's easily wronged and offended; and it bears grudges against those who don't think like it, look like it, or act like it. (3) It's *touchy*. It's like a bone out of joint. It won't allow anyone near it. When confronted, it will deflect attention. It plays the vic-

---

[3] See 1 Peter 2:11.
[4] Quoted in Thomas, *A Puritan Golden Treasury*, 223.
[5] Jonathan Edwards, *Charity and Its Fruits: Christian Love as Manifested in the Heart and Life* (1852; rep., Edinburgh: Banner of Truth, 2000), 112.

tim—always wronged, always misunderstood, always offended. Edwards warns, "An envious Christian, a malicious Christian, a cold and hard-hearted Christian, is the greatest absurdity and contradiction. It is as if one should speak of dark brightness, or a false truth."[6]

Because of conceit, we're tempted to attach our desire to be uppermost to things—wealth, beauty, ability, and family; even spiritual gifts, causes, and ministries—thereby turning these things into idols. They become conditions for friendship and fellowship. They become standards by which we judge others. We expect others to pay allegiance to our idols. What happens if they don't? Envy quickly morphs into contempt and disdain, and all hell breaks loose (Jas. 3:15).

Provoking One Another
Conceit also leads to "provoking one another." James tells us that frustrated "selfish ambition" leads to "bitter jealousy," which in turn leads to "disorder and every vile practice" (Jas. 3:16). God established order at creation. Satan hates it, and his goal is to sow chaos and confusion. The chief way he does so is by stirring up envy.

We see it in the case of Cain and Abel. God is pleased with Abel's sacrifice, but he's displeased with Cain's. "Cain becomes very angry and his countenance falls" (Gen. 4:5). His envy leads to "disorder and every vile practice."

We see it in the case of Joseph and his brothers. Joseph has a dream, depicting his brothers bowing before him. "They hate him even more for his dreams and for his words" (Gen. 37:8). Their envy leads to "disorder and every vile practice."

We see it in the case of David and Saul. "Saul has slain his thousands, and David his ten thousands." Saul can't bear it. "Saul looks at David with suspicion from that day on" (1 Sam. 18:9). His envy leads to "disorder and every vile practice."

We see it in the case of Haman and Mordecai. The king honors Mordecai. "When Haman sees Mordecai … he's filled with anger against him" (Esth. 5:9). His envy leads to "disorder and every vile practice."

---

[6] Edwards, *Charity and Its Fruits*, 23.

We see it in the case of Daniel and his colleagues. "The king planned to appoint him over the entire kingdom" (Dan. 6:3–4). Their envy leads to "disorder and every vile practice."

We see it in the case of Christ and the Jewish leaders. They don't possess his authority. They can't preach and teach like him. They can't challenge his wisdom. They envy Christ. Their envy leads to "disorder and every vile practice."

Envy might not lead to anything quite as extreme as the cases above, but it will cause us to find ways to punish those who refuse to surrender to our desire to be uppermost. (1) We might use our *expressions*. We smirk and snarl, we huff and puff, we pout and glare. We roll our eyes and shake our heads. (2) We might use our *actions*. At times, we use intimidation; we seek to get our way through angry outbursts. At other times, we use isolation; we seek to get our way by withdrawing. Coldness and aloofness become our weapons of choice. (3) We might use our *words*. Our words become harsh, dismissive, careless, thoughtless, malicious, slanderous, sarcastic, and negative. We criticize and bicker. We use our words to cut and bite. "The tongue is a fire ... set on fire by hell" (Jas. 3:6).

We use each of these things to communicate a simple message: "I wish you were dead." It can happen in marriages, families, friendships, communities, and churches. There's distance where once there was closeness, suspicion where once there was trust, animosity where once there was compassion, accusation where once there was encouragement, avoidance where once there was openness, bitterness where once there was sweetness. At the root of it all lies *conceit*.

Conclusion

What is the remedy? Paul has already told us: we must keep in step with the Spirit (5:25). We do so by remembering that "those who belong to Christ Jesus have crucified the flesh with its passions and desires" (5:24). By the knowledge of God's greatness, we see our smallness (Judg. 6:22). By the knowledge of God holiness, we see our sinfulness (Isa. 6:5). By the knowledge of God's loving-kindness, we see our unworthiness. "I know that nothing good dwells in me" (Rom. 7:18). "I am the least of the apostles" (1 Cor. 15:9). "I am nothing" (2 Cor. 12:11). "I am the very least of all the saints" (Eph. 3:8). "I am the foremost sinner" (1 Tim. 1:15).

Avoiding Conceit (5:26)

When we live in the light of the gospel, we put "conceit" to death. As the Word of God (the Spirit of God) dwells in us, we're conformed to Christ's likeness: love, joy, peace, patience, kindness, goodness, faithfulness, gentleness, and self-control (5:22). This fruit is manifested in our choices, pursuits, actions, and words. It isn't contentious, but dispels grudges, rivalries, and factions. It promotes peace and longs for unity. It's thoughtful and generous in its dealings with others. It's open to reason, responding to authority and yielding to persuasion. It responds thoughtfully to questions and arguments; and it is willing to comply. It acts generously and compassionately to others, especially those in need. It shows itself in action.

As "the fruit of the Spirit" pushes out "the works of the flesh," what happens? There's peace. As James says, "A harvest of righteousness is sown in peace by those who make peace" (Jas. 3:18). James probably has the Hebrew concept of shalom in mind—wholeness. It's when everything is right—as it should be. A day is coming when shalom will reign throughout the universe. James's point is that those who live in the meekness of wisdom catch a foretaste of shalom in their present relationships.

21
The Fruit of the Spirit in Action: Bearing Burdens (6:1-5)

Is there something more to the Christian life? Some look to a decisive experience that leads to the higher life or victorious life; they speak of a complete filling, total breaking, or second blessing. Some look to a particular calling as holding out hope of a closer walk with God; they turn to the martyr, mystic, monastic, missionary, or minister, as exemplifying some sort of super spirituality. Some look to detachment from everyday life as essential to spiritual progress; they think that release from the mundane roles and responsibilities of life will free them to pursue a deeper relationship with God.

Paul has a very different view of the Christian life. He has demonstrated that we're simply called to live as those who belong to Christ (2:20; 5:24). Doing so means keeping in step with the Spirit (5:25). As the fruit of the Spirit takes hold in our lives, it forces out the works of the flesh. To put it another way, self-less love replaces selfish love (5:26).

As Paul now demonstrates, this is especially important when it comes to two specific situations in the churches of Galatia. The first is the subject of this chapter. "Bear one another's burdens," says Paul, "and so fulfill the law of Christ" (6:2). There are many ways to carry other people's burdens. There are physical burdens such as illness. There are emotional burdens such as bereavement. There are financial burdens such as unemployment. When we "bear" one another's burdens, we fulfill the law of Christ; that is, we love as Christ loved (5:14).

In the context, Paul is thinking primarily of the burden of sin: "Brothers, if anyone is caught in any transgression, you who are spiritual should restore him in a spirit of gentleness" (6:1). The term "restore" (*katartizdo*) is used of rebuilding walls (Ezra 4:12-13) and mending nets (Matt. 4:21). It sounds pleasant, but it isn't. It's often akin to putting a dislocated bone back in place. In other words, there's pain before there's relief. Paul entrusts the restoration of sinners to those who bear three marks.

The Spiritual (6:1)

"You who are spiritual ..." What does it mean to be spiritual? Some look to special experiences of the gifts of the Spirit in prayer and worship; the more exceptional the experience the more convinced they are of the Spirit's working. Some look to learning; they equate knowing God with reading books, mastering doctrine, and dabbling in speculative theology. Some look to causes, methods, movements, or ideologies; they think these entail a deeper understanding of the Christian faith and evidence a closer walk with God. Some look to celebratory events, retreats, or conferences; they believe God works in a special way when there are great crowds, great music, and great exuberance. Some look to a mystical experience; they believe that knowing God transcends words and thoughts, and they long for a bare communion of the soul with God.

All these notions of the "spiritual" life are fallacies. Simply put, to be spiritual is to be "led" by the Spirit (5:18) and to "live" by the Spirit (5:25). The adjective "spiritual" is used in the NT for those things that are the result of the Holy Spirit's action.[1] Thus, the NT term "spiritual" is quite different from its modern usage. It doesn't refer to things that are immaterial as opposed to material (or corporeal), nor does it refer to the soul, as the spiritual part of man, in opposition to the body, which is the material part. Instead, the term "spiritual" refers to that which is related to the Holy Spirit. "It is with relation to the Holy Ghost, or Spirit of God, that persons or things are termed spiritual, in the New Testament. 'Spirit,' as the word is used to signify the third person in the Trinity, is the substantive, of which is formed the adjective 'spiritual,' in the Holy Scriptures."[2] What does this mean for spirituality? Richard Lovelace tells us: "True spirituality is not a superhuman religiosity; it is simply true humanity released from bondage to sin and renewed by the Holy Spirit."[3] It's to be born again.

---

[1] See "spiritual truths" (1 Cor. 2:13), "spiritual things" (1 Cor. 9:11), "spiritual wisdom" (Col. 1:9), "spiritual gifts" (1 Cor. 12:1; 14:1), "spiritual songs" (Eph. 5:19; Col. 3:16), "spiritual blessings" (Eph. 1:3), "spiritual house" (1 Pet. 2:5), "spiritual sacrifices" (1 Pet. 2:5), and "spiritual people" (1 Cor. 2:15; 3:1).

[2] Edwards, *Religious Affections*, 198.

[3] Richard Lovelace, *Dynamics of Spiritual Life: An Evangelical Theology of Renewal* (Downers Grove: Inter-Varsity, 1979), 19.

The Gentle (6:1)

"In a spirit of gentleness ..." When faced with a sinning brother, we might be tempted to ignore him—to sit in pious judgment, deriving quiet satisfaction from his sin; or, we might be tempted to despise him and look upon him with disdain; or, we might be tempted to attack—to make public what should remain private, and to denounce openly rather than rebuke quietly. Such responses are "the works of the flesh." Ultimately, they're manifestations of self-love, not selfless love.

But those who are "led" by the Spirit also "walk" by the Spirit. The evidence is seen in the fruit of the Spirit—gentleness (5:23).[4] Christ's gentleness is evident in the way he deals with the poor in spirit. He doesn't break off the "battered reed" or put out the "smoldering wick" (Matt. 12:20). Instead, he calls, "Come to me, all who are weary and heavy-laden, and I will give you rest" (Matt. 11:28). He invites to himself those who bear the burden of their sin, guilt, and shame. He won't break a bruised reed because he's full of sympathy: "The Lord is full of compassion and is merciful" (Jas. 5:11). He won't extinguish a smoldering wick because he's full of compassion: "He heals the brokenhearted and binds up their wounds" (Ps. 147:3).

Likewise, we're to be gentle toward others. "But we proved to be gentle among you," says Paul, "as a nursing mother tenderly cares for her own children" (1 Thess. 2:7). We must be gentle when it comes to doctrinal error: "With gentleness correcting those who are in opposition, if perhaps God may grant them repentance leading to the knowledge of the truth" (2 Tim. 2:25). And we must be gentle when it comes to moral failure: "Brothers, if anyone is caught in any transgression, you who are spiritual should restore him in a spirit of gentleness" (6:1).

The Watchful (6:2-5)

"Keep watch on yourself ..." The term "watch" means to be alert to the threat of danger.[5] The mariner needs to watch for rocks and reefs. The hiker needs to watch for snakes. The pilot needs to watch for storms. The soldier needs to watch for enemies. When danger lurks, carelessness is costly.

The devil is on the prowl; the world is at the door; and the flesh is actively opposing all that's of the Spirit. We must watch for these three enemies. With great urgency, we must watch our own hearts. "Keep your heart with

---

[4] See Paul's example of gentleness in 3:1 and 4:19-20.
[5] See Acts 20:31; 1 Peter 5:8; Revelation 3:2.

all vigilance, for from it flow the springs of life" (Prov. 4:23). Our heart is the seat of our personality—our mind and will. We must keep it "with all vigilance." When we put out the garbage on a Tuesday night, we don't guard it. As a matter of fact, we don't give it another thought. Why? It's worthless. We only guard what we value. The heart is valuable because "from it flows the springs of life." A spring is an opening in the ground where water (from below the surface) discharges. It accumulates in pools or streams. If you stop a spring, what happens? The stream is stopped. If you poison a spring, what happens? The stream is poisoned. What happens to the spring determines what happens to the stream. The same is true of the heart. Our words, attitudes, and actions are all determined by our heart. The condition of our heart determines the condition of our life.

Watchfulness means we must examine ourselves. "If anyone thinks he is something, when he is nothing, he deceives himself. But let each one test his own work, and then his reason to boast will be in himself alone and not in his neighbor. For each will have to bear his own load" (6:3–5). Admittedly, these verses are a little tricky. Paul seems to be referring to what he said in 5:26, "Let us not become conceited, provoking one another, envying one another." His point is that conceit will prevent us from bearing other people's burdens. A superiority complex will cause us to seek confrontation; we think we're better than others, and we're happy to engage in situations that reenforce our self-delusion. To avoid the threat posed by conceit, we must not compare ourselves to others but evaluate ourselves—"test [our] own work." Moreover, we must remember that we'll "bear [our] own load" on the judgement day.

Conclusion

The burden of sin is a heavy load to bear. "When I kept silent," David declares, "my bones wasted away through my groaning all day long. For day and night your hand was heavy upon me; my strength was dried" (Ps. 32:3–4). David strayed in spectacular fashion and, as a result, he lost the enjoyment of God. This loss impacted him, in that he felt like a bone-out-of-joint. Those who wander are usually out of sorts. They detach themselves from others, to avoid exposure. They adopt a critical spirit, to mask their own spiritual condition. They assume a victim mentality, to place themselves beyond scrutiny. They're often characterized by surliness, aloofness, and coldness. They're greatly burdened.

This is when selfless love steps in. Those who are spiritual, gentle, and watchful (that is, those who are keeping in step with the Spirit) seek to restore the transgressor. Our message is simple: we proclaim that there is forgiveness for those weighed down by the burden of sin. We can do no better than point the sinner to David's words: "Have mercy on me, O God, according to your steadfast love; according to your abundant mercy blot out my transgressions" (Ps. 51:2).

> Oh, to grace how great a debtor,
> Daily I'm constrained to be
> Let your goodness like a fetter,
> Bind my wandering heart to thee
> Prone to wander, Lord I feel it,
> Prone to leave the God I love
> Here's my heart, Lord, take and seal it,
> Seal it for thy courts above.[6]

---

[6] Robert Robinson, "Come, Thou Fount of Every Blessing" (hymn).

22

The Fruit of the Spirit in Action: Doing Good (6:6–10)

Christ offered himself upon Calvary's cross to make atonement for sin. God now offers Christ to sinners for their salvation. Upon receiving Christ through faith, we're implanted into him. We take possession of all the benefits and blessings that are found in him. We become the righteousness of God in Christ (2 Cor. 5:21). Now, we seek to live out our identity in Christ (5:24). This means that the gospel is about being God's people in everyday life, and that's one of the things that makes Paul's Epistle to the Galatians so compelling. This isn't esoteric philosophy or speculative theology. In this letter, we see how the gospel breaks into every sphere of life. It informs us, challenges us, and shapes us. In the last chapter, we saw that it compels us to bear others' burdens; in this, we see that it compels us to meet others' needs.

In a word, we're to "do good to everyone" (6:10). Goodness is numbered among the fruit of the Spirit (5:22). We "do good" when we're mindful of the needs of others and meet those needs according to our own resources and abilities. Mindful of the body, we seek to meet people's *physical* needs. Mindful of the soul, we seek to meet people's *spiritual* needs. We're like Christ who was "moved with compassion" for the multitudes because they were "as sheep having no shepherd" (Matt. 9:36).[1]

The Bible has a great deal to say about *doing good*. For starters, the purpose of Christ's death is "to redeem us and to purify for himself a people for his own possession who are zealous for good deeds" (Titus 2:14). We are God's "workmanship, created in Christ Jesus for good works, which [he] prepared beforehand, that we should walk in them" (Eph. 2:10). These "good works" are the evidence of salvation (2 Tim. 1:9; Jas. 2:14–26). Therefore, we're "to be rich in good works" (1 Tim. 6:18); we're to be "ready for every good work" (2 Tim. 2:21; Titus 3:1); we're to be "a model of good works" (Titus 2:7); and we're to "devote [ourselves] to good

---

[1] Christ is also "moved with compassion" when he sees the sick (Matt. 14:14), the hungry (Matt. 15:32), and the blind (Matt. 20:34).

works" (Titus 3:8, 14). As a result, unbelievers will "see [our] good deeds and glorify God on the day of visitation" (1 Pet. 2:12).

What do we learn about *doing good* from what Paul writes in 6:6-10?

A Precept (6:6)

"Let the one who is taught the word share all good things with the one who teaches." Clearly, we're to give to the work of the ministry, and we're to view this giving as an act of fellowship. Elsewhere, Paul says that those "who rule well" are worthy of "double honor" (1 Tim. 5:17-18). To "rule well" is to labour in preaching and teaching. The word "labour" (*kopiao*) signifies working to the point of fatigue or exhaustion. We have a good example of what that looks like in 1 Timothy 4:6-16, where Paul tells Timothy to devote himself to the public reading, preaching, and teaching of Scripture. Among the elders in a local church, there might be those who expend themselves in God's Word. They're ruling well and, therefore, are worthy of double honour. All elders are to receive honour, but those elders who labour in the Word are to receive double honour. The word "honour" has a twofold meaning: reward (1 Tim. 5:3) and respect (1 Tim. 6:1).

A Principle (6:7-8)

"Do not be deceived: God is not mocked, for whatever one sows, that will he also reap. For the one who sows to his own flesh will from the flesh reap corruption, but the one who sows to the Spirit will from the Spirit reap eternal life." We reap what we sow because we live in a moral universe. God has designed it to be so. If we eat junk food, we experience poor health. If we neglect our relationships, we alienate people. If we speed in icy weather, we skid off the road. You get the idea. The same is true in the spiritual realm. If we sow to "the flesh," we reap "corruption"—eternal death. If, however, we sow to the Spirit, we reap "eternal life."

How do we "sow to the Spirit"? We belong to Christ, meaning we've "crucified the flesh with its passions and desires" (5:24). We're one with him in his death, burial, and resurrection. This is a positional reality. It's also a transformational reality because we're now "led" by the Spirit (5:18) and we now "live by the Spirit" (5:25). Consequently, we seek to keep in step with the Spirit (5:25). As we do, the fruit of the Spirit (5:22-23) pushes out the "desires" and "works" of the flesh (5:16, 19). Selfish love gives way to self-less love (5:26), and this now shapes our relationships—specifically, how we carry the burdens and meet the needs of others (6:1-10).

This is what it means to "sow to the Spirit." It isn't the meritorious cause of salvation, but it most certainly is the demonstrable evidence of salvation. That's why Paul says that those who "sow to the Spirit" reap "eternal life." It's the way to eternal life because it's the way God has ordained for those who are in Christ to walk.

A Promise (6:9-10)

"And let us not grow weary of doing good, for in due season we will reap, if we do not give up. So then, as we have opportunity, let us do good to everyone, and especially to those who are of the household of faith." Doing good can lead to weariness.[2] But Paul offers a word of encouragement: there will be a harvest. There will be a harvest in the lives of others and in our own lives. There will be a harvest in the future because we will reap eternal life. We'll hear our Saviour say, "Well done good and faithful servant" (Matt. 25:23).

For this reason, we aren't to "give up." Instead, we're to do good to everyone, especially those who belong to the household of faith. The term "household" (*oikiakos*) refers to the church.[3] She stands at the centre of God's eternal plans and purposes. She's the eternal magnifying of his glorious grace, immeasurable power, and manifold wisdom. She's the bride and body of Christ, and she's Christ's visible form in the world, meaning she reflects his splendor, manifests his glory, displays his beauty, and mirrors his holiness. She exemplifies godliness amid ungodliness, love amid hate, order amid chaos, forgiveness amid bitterness, compassion amid selfishness, peace amid hostility.

We should be looking for ways "to do good" to our fellow members in the body of Christ. Jonathan Edwards writes, "Let our benevolence and beneficence be universal, constant, free, habitual, and according to our opportunities and ability; for this is essential to true piety and required by the commands of God."[4] Moving beyond "the household of faith," says Paul, we're to "do good to everyone." We must not restrict *doing good* to acts of serving the poor, helping the sick, visiting the infirm, etc. (although it cer-

---

[2] See 2 Thessalonians 3:13.
[3] See Ephesians 2:19.
[4] Edwards, *Charity and Its Fruits*, 106.

tainly includes these things), but see it as the natural outworking of the faithful performance of our callings. God has placed each of us in a particular calling (1 Cor. 7:17). When we fulfill our vocation in a God-honouring manner, we perform those "good works which God prepared beforehand that we should walk in them" (Eph. 2:10). This is the case because the faithful execution of our vocation contributes to the common good—the betterment of society. It is, therefore, the chief means by which we express our love for God and neighbour (Mark 12:30–31).

God has assigned us and called us to a life—single or married, carpenter or electrician, student or retiree, government official or manual labourer, parent or child, etc. We "do good" by living out our identity in Christ in whatever calling God has appointed for us.

Conclusion

"You are good and do good" (Ps. 119:68). How does our God manifest his goodness toward us? He manifests it in creation: "And God saw everything that he had made, and behold, it was very good" (Gen. 1:31). He manifests it in providence: "The LORD is good to all, and his mercy is over all he has made" (Ps. 145:9). Most importantly, he manifests it in redemption: "But when the goodness and loving kindness of God our Saviour appeared, he saved us, not because of works done by us in righteousness, but according to his own mercy" (Titus 3:4). Christ is the full manifestation of God's goodness. He demonstrates it by healing the sick, freeing the demoniac, and raising the dead. He proclaims it by willingly laying down his life to ransom sinners.

Christ's claims are full of goodness. "I am the light of the world" (John 8:12). "I am the way, the truth, and the life" (John 14:6). "I am the bread of life" (John 6:35). "I am the good Shepherd. The good shepherd lays down his life for the sheep" (John 10:11). "I came that they may have life and have it abundantly" (John 10:10).

Christ's promises are full of goodness. "Whoever comes to me shall not hunger, and whoever believers in me shall never thirst" (John 6:35). "Whoever comes to me I will never cast out" (John 6:37). "Whoever believes in me, as the Scripture has said, 'Out of his heart will flow rivers of living water'" (John 7:38). "Whoever follows me will not walk in darkness but will have the light of life" (John 8:12).Christ brings "good news to the poor" (Luke 4:18). What makes it "good" is that it corresponds to our greatest need. If I have a broken arm, I don't need cough medicine. If I have bronchitis, I don't need a cast on my leg. If I have cataracts, I don't need a knee replacement. If I'm a sinner who stands condemned in God's sight, I don't need self-help recipes or how-to seminars. I need a Saviour. The good news is that we don't need to earn our way to God because Christ has earned it for us. The good news is that, because of Christ, God is willing to say to us: "Your sins are forgiven" (Luke 7:48). His forgiveness isn't conditional, nor is it a process. God forgives instantly, completely, and freely. "He heals the broken hearted and binds up their wounds" (Ps. 147:3). The gospel extends great hope, for where there's conviction for sin, God promises mercy; where there's weariness for sin, he promises rest; where there's repentance for sin, he promises forgiveness. As William Gurnall so eloquently puts it: "It is impossible for him to reject a poor penitent sinner, merely for the greatness of the sins he has committed ... He promises pardon to poor sinners."[5] God is good.

---

[5] William Gurnall, *The Christian in Complete Armor: A Treatise of the Saints' War against the Devil* (1662-1665; London: Blackie & Son, 1864; rpt., Edinburgh: Banner of Truth, 1995), 505.

Conclusion

23
Lasting Impressions (6:11–18)

We've come to the end of our study of Paul's Epistle to the Galatians. You will recall that, during his first missionary journey, Paul planted churches in the region of Galatia. At a subsequent point, he received word that all was not well in these churches. Troublemakers were undermining his ministry, alleging that he wasn't a real apostle—or, at least, not an apostle on the same level as the "pillars" at Jerusalem. They also suggested that Paul had corrupted the gospel he had received from the apostles by failing to preach that observance of the OT law was necessary for salvation.

In this letter, Paul responds by defending (1) the authority of his ministry, and (2) the accuracy of his message. His argument unfolds as follows:

Salutation (1:1–5)
Caution (1:6–10)

Paul defends the authority of his mission:
    (1) The Gospel "Revealed" (1:11–2:14)
    (2) The Gospel "Explained" (2:15–21)

Paul defends the accuracy of his message:
(3) The Gospel "Defended" (3:1–5:12)
(4) The Gospel "Applied" (5:13–6:10)

Caution (6:11–17)
Benediction (6:18)

Paul begins to draw his letter to a close by turning his readers' attention to the obvious change in handwriting. "See with what large letters I am writing to you with my own hand" (6:11). To this point, he has been dictating and a scribe has been writing. But now, he takes the reed pen in hand, and he writes these concluding words in large letters. Why? If we want to emphasize a sentence in an email, we might write the letters in upper case, highlight them in bold, and underline them. This makes them stand out to the reader.

This seems to be what Paul is doing. He wants his final words to make a lasting impression. In particular, he wants to focus his readers' attention on two pivotal truths that, if rightly understood, would resolve the entire controversy among the Galatian churches.

The Sufficiency of Christ (6:12–14)

The first concerns the meritorious cause of salvation. Paul takes up this theme at the very outset of his letter, declaring that Christ "gave himself for our sins to deliver us from the present evil age" (1:4). He addresses it in detail in 2:15–21, explaining that we're justified "through faith in Christ." Christ is the meritorious cause while faith is the instrumental means of justification. Christ alone is a sufficient Saviour because he has "redeemed us from the curse of the law by becoming a curse for us" (3:13). Paul again emphasizes this truth in 4:4–5, teaching that "when the fullness of time had come, God sent forth his Son, born of woman, born under the law, to redeem those who were under the law, so that we might receive adoption as sons."

Now, as he concludes his letter, Paul speaks one more time to the sole sufficiency of Christ. He says that those who insist on living under the law do so "in order that they may not be persecuted for the cross of Christ" (6:12). In addition, they do so because they want to "boast in [their] flesh" (6:13). They're convinced that they can earn God's favour by means of their ethnicity and religiosity. They believe human effort is a meritorious cause of salvation.

In sharp contrast, Paul says that he boasts "in the cross of our Lord Jesus Christ" (6:14). God reckoned our guilt to Christ upon the cross, and he annulled the law when Christ satisfied its demand of perfect obedience, bore its curse, and fulfilled its shadows, types, and ceremonies. It was nailed to the cross with Christ, and it died when he died. Because of our union with Christ, we can say with Paul: "the world has been crucified to me, and I to the world" (6:14). We're dead to it, meaning it no longer has any control or influence upon us.

Elsewhere, Paul writes, "But whatever gain I had, I counted as loss for the sake of Christ. Indeed, I count everything as loss because of the surpassing worth of knowing Christ Jesus my Lord" (Phil. 3:7–8). Here Paul counts two things as "loss." First, he counts as "loss for the sake of Christ" whatever "gain" he had. Here, he's referring to his self-righteousness (Phil. 3:4–6). It's worthless in comparison to Christ. Second, he counts "everything as loss because of the surpassing worth of knowing Christ Jesus." Here Paul has more than his self-righteousness in view. He's saying that he counts all things as rubbish in comparison to the surpassing worth of knowing Christ.

When we boast in the cross, we're saying that Christ does it all. He takes our sin, and he achieves righteousness in his obedience. We simply receive him (and all his benefits) through faith. Faith does nothing. It pays nothing, earns nothing, and contributes nothing. It simply receives. Do we believe that Christ was crucified for us—that he stood in our place while our sins were applied to him? As we hear of Christ agonizing in the garden, do we think of our sins that brought such pain upon him? As we hear of Christ's condemnation before Pilate, do we marvel at God's infinite mercy toward sinners? As we hear of Christ naked upon the cross, do we remember that he covers our shame with his righteousness? As we hear of Christ's cry from the cross, do we think of how he suffered the torment of hell in our place? As we hear of the trembling of the earth, do we think of how we deserved to descend to hell? This is to believe in a sufficient Saviour.

> Nothing in my hand I bring,
> Simply to thy cross I cling.
> Naked, come to thee for dress,
> Helpless, look to thee for grace.
> Foul, I to the Fountain fly;
> Wash me, Saviour, or I die.[1]

The Identity of Israel (6:15–16)

The second theme concerns the people of God. Who are they? Paul also takes up this theme when he declares that Christ "gave himself for our sins to deliver us from the present evil age" (1:4). The implication is that Christ has inaugurated something new. "In Christ Jesus the blessing of Abraham [has] come to the Gentiles, so that we might receive the promised Spirit through faith" (3:9). Christ has baptized us with his Spirit into his body and, therefore, we have "put on Christ" (3:27). For Paul, the implication is that we're all "one in Christ Jesus" (3:28). Because we belong to Christ, we're all "Abraham's offspring, heirs according to promise" (3:29). As Paul states in 5:6, "For in Christ Jesus neither circumcision nor uncircumcision counts for anything, but only faith working through love."

---

[1] Augustus Toplady, "Rock of Ages, Cleft for Me" (hymn).

In his conclusion, Paul returns to this central truth: "For neither circumcision counts for anything, nor uncircumcision, but a new creation" (6:15). As far as he's concerned, circumcision (being a Jew) and uncircumcision (being a Gentile) are irrelevant—that is to say, man's effort is irrelevant. The only thing that matters is that we're part of the new creation. Christ's crucifixion and resurrection mark its beginning. We've received the Holy Spirit, and we've been delivered from the present evil age. Now, we live in the present age as those who belong to the age to come.

"And as for all who walk by this rule, peace and mercy be upon them, and upon the Israel of God" (6:16).[2] What does Paul mean by "the Israel of God"? As Thomas Schreiner acknowledges, "It would be highly confusing to the Galatians, after arguing for the equality of Jew and Gentile in Christ (3:28), and after emphasizing that believers are Abraham's children, for Paul to argue in the conclusion that only Jews who believe in Jesus belong to the Israel of God."[3] This is precisely what some Jews in the churches of Galatia are teaching, thereby implying that Gentile believers don't belong to the people of God. Paul's response is scandalous. He informs these Jews that they aren't real Jews—they aren't the true Israel. Christ is the true Israel. He's the promised seed of Abraham. He's the fulfillment of the Abrahamic covenant. He's the heir of all the Abrahamic promises. Because believers (Jews and Gentiles) are one with Christ, they are "Abraham's offspring, heirs according to promise" (3:29). They're "the Israel of God."

As Greg Beale explains, "Christ is the true Israel, and as true Israel, he represents the church as the continuation of true Israel from the OT. Christ came to do what Israel should have done but failed to do. Those who identify by faith with Christ (whether Jew or Gentile) become identified with him and his identity as true eschatological Israel."[4] The true Israel isn't the nation of Israel under the old covenant. It's Christ—the true Prophet, Priest, and King. Christ is Israel, in that God's purposes and promises for the nation are fulfilled in him, and this fulfillment is extended to his spiritual body—the church. The calling of God's people from among the Gentiles is the promised restoration of Israel because the church is the continuation of the believ-

---

[2] The term "walk" (*stoikeo*) is also found in 5:25. For the link between Paul's blessing of "peace and mercy" and the new creation language of Isaiah 54:8-10, see Fesko, *Galatians*, 207-8.

[3] Schreiner, *Galatians*, 383.

[4] Greg Beale, *A New Testament Biblical Theology: The Unfolding of the Old Testament in the New* (Ada: Baker Academic, 2011), 652.

ing remnant with ethnic Israel. The Gentiles, therefore, are no longer "strangers and aliens," but "fellow citizens with the saints and members of the household of God" (Eph. 2:19). The categories of Jew and Gentile are now irrelevant. Believing Jews and Gentiles constitute a "new creation" — Christ and his church.[5]

Conclusion

Paul has presented his case, refuting those who question his authority, rebuking those who corrupt the gospel, and encouraging those in danger of falling away. "From now on let no one cause me trouble, for I bear on my body the marks of Jesus" (6:17).[6] To this, he adds a simple prayer: "The grace of our Lord Jesus Christ be with your spirit, brothers. Amen" (6:18).[7] Here he reiterates the fundamental issue that he has sought to resolve for the Galatians in this letter: grace comes from Christ because he is an all-sufficient Saviour.

> As the eye seeks for no other light than that of the sun and joins no candles with it to dishonour the sufficiency of its beams, so no created thing must be joined to Christ as an object of faith. This is a dishonour to the strength of this Rock, which is our only foundation ... It is a folly to seek for security anywhere else ... We cannot trust him too much, nor ourselves too little.[8]

---

[5] God refers to the church as his beloved (Rom. 9:25; 1 Thess. 1:4). See Deuteronomy 32:15; 33:12; Isaiah 44:2; Jeremiah 11:15; 12:7. God refers to the church as his son (Gal. 3:26). See Exodus 4:22-23; Deuteronomy 14:1; Isaiah 1:2; 63:8; Hosea 1:10; 11:1. God refers to the church as his bride (2 Cor. 11:2; Eph. 5:25-27). See Isaiah 54:5-6; Ezekiel 16:32; Hosea 1:2. God refers to the church as his vineyard (John 15:1-5; 1 Cor. 3:9). See Isaiah 5:1-7; Jeremiah 12:10. God refers to the church as his special people (Titus 2:14). See Exodus 19:5; 23:22; Deuteronomy 7:6; 14:2. God refers to the church as a kingdom of priests (1 Pet. 2:9; Rev. 1:6; 5:10). See Exodus 19:6.

[6] See 2 Corinthians 11:24-27

[7] For "grace," see 1:3, 6, 15; 2:9, 21; 5:4.

[8] Stephen Charnock, *The Complete Works of Stephen Charnock*, 5 vols (Edinburgh: Banner of Truth, 1997), 5:176.

About the Author

Dr. J. Stephen Yuille has been married to Alison since 1991. They have two daughters, Laura and Emma. Dr. Yuille has over twenty years of ministry experience, including serving as a missionary in Portugal, pastoring churches in Ontario and Texas, and teaching at several colleges and seminaries. He is the professor of pastoral theology and spiritual formation at Southwestern Baptist Theological Seminary in Fort Worth, Texas. In addition to publishing books and articles related to English Puritanism, he has authored several popular works, including: *A Hope Deferred: Adoption and the Fatherhood of God*; *Longing for Home: A Journey Through the Psalms of Ascent*; *The Path of Life: Blessedness in Seasons of Lament*; *The Obedience of Faith: Paul's Epistle to the Romans*.

Bibliography

Alleine, Joseph. *A Sure Guide to Heaven*. 1672; rpt., London: Banner of Truth, 1989.

Augustine, *On Christian Doctrine*, 1:5, in *Nicene and Post-Nicene Fathers*, vol 2, ed. Phillip Schaff. Peabody: Hendrickson, 1990.

Barna, George. *Third Millennium Teens*. Ventura: The Barna Research Group, 1999.

Baxter, Richard. *The Practical Works of Rev. Richard Baxter*. London: James Duncan, 1830.

Baxter, Richard. *The Practical Works of Richard Baxter: Select Treatises*. Grand Rapids: Baker Books, 1981.

Beale, Greg. *A New Testament Biblical Theology: The Unfolding of the Old Testament in the New*. Ada: Baker Academic, 2011.

Bray, Gerald. "Union and Communion: Joining the Fellowship of Heaven," in *For All the Saints: Evangelical Theology and Christian Spirituality*, eds. Timothy George and Alister McGrath. Louisville: Westminster John Knox Press, 2003.

Bonar, Andrew. *Memoir and Remains of Robert Murray M'Cheyne*. Edinburgh: Oliphant, Anderson, and Ferrier, 1883.

Brown, John. *An Exposition of the Epistle to the Galatians*. Evansville: The Sovereign Grace Book Club, 1957.

Bruce, F. F. *The Epistle to the Galatians*, in *The New International Greek Testament Commentary*. Grand Rapids: Eerdmans, 1990.

Bunyan, John. *A Discourse upon the Pharisee and the Publican*, in *The Miscellaneous Works of John Bunyan*, vol 10, ed. Owen Watkins. Oxford: Clarendon Press, 1988

Bunyan, John. *A Treatise on the Fear of God*. London, 1679; rpt. Morgan: Soli Deo Gloria, 1999.

Bunyan, John. *Grace Abounding to the Chief of Sinners*. Middlesex: Echo Library, 2006.

Calvin, John. *Institutes of the Christian Religion*, in *The Library of Christian Classics*, vols 20–21, ed. J. T. McNeill. Philadelphia: Westminster Press, 1960.

Chapple, Allan. *True Devotion: In Search of Authentic Spirituality*. London: The Latimer Trust, 2014.

Charnock, Stephen. *The Complete Works of Stephen Charnock*, 5 vols. Edinburgh: Banner of Truth, 1997.

Dunn, James. *The Theology of Paul the Apostle*. Grand Rapids: Eerdmans, 1998.

Edwards, Jonathan. *Charity and Its Fruits: Christian Love as Manifested in the Heart and Life*. 1852; rpt., Edinburgh: Banner of Truth, 2000.

Edwards, Jonathan. *The Religious Affections*. Edinburgh: Banner of Truth, 1961.

Edwards, Jonathan. *The Works of Jonathan Edwards*, 2 vols. 1834; rpt., Peabody: Hendrickson, 1998.

Flavel, John. *Christ and His Threefold Office*, ed. J. Stephen Yuille. Grand Rapids: Reformation Heritage Books, 2021.

Flavel, John. *The Works of John Flavel*, 6 vols. London: Banner of Truth, 1968.

Fesko, J. V. *Galatians*, in *The Lectio Continua Series*. Powder Springs: Tolle Lege Press, 2012.

Gaffin, Richard B. *By Faith, Not By Sight: Paul and the Order of Salvation*. Wanesboro: Paternoster, 2006.

Garlington, Don. *An Exposition of Galatians: A Reading from the New Perspective*. Eugene: Wipf & Stock, 2007.

George, Timothy. *Galatians*, in *The New American Commentary*. Nashville: Broadman & Holman, 1994.

Goodwin, Thomas. *The Works of Thomas Goodwin*. 1861; rpt., Grand Rapids: Reformation Heritage Books, 2006.

Goldsworthy, Graeme. *According to Plan: The Unfolding Revelation of God in the Bible*. Downers Grove: Inter-Varsity Press, 1991.

Gurnall, William. *The Christian in Complete Armor: A Treatise of the Saints' War against the Devil*. 1662–1665; London: Blackie & Son, 1864; rpt., Edinburgh: Banner of Truth, 1995.

Haykin, Michael. *Rediscovering the Church Fathers: Who They Were and How They Shaped the Church*. Wheaton: Crossway, 2011.

Hendriksen, William. *New Testament Commentary: Exposition of Galatians.* Grand Rapids: Baker Books, 2007.

Lewis, C. S. *Mere Christianity.* San Francisco: Harper, 2015.

Lightfoot, J. B. *The Epistle of St. Paul to the Galatians*, in *Classic Commentary Library.* Grand Rapids: Zondervan, 1957.

Lovelace, Richard. *Dynamics of Spiritual Life: An Evangelical Theology of Renewal.* Downers Grove: Inter-Varsity, 1979.

Luther, Martin. *A Commentary on St Paul's Epistle to the Galatians.* Cambridge: James Clarke, 1953.

Luther, Martin. *Luther's Works*, 55 vols, ed. H. T. Lehmann. Philadelphia: Fortress Press, 1957.

MacDonald, William. *Believers Bible Commentary—New Testament.* Nashville: Thomas Nelson, 1989.

Manickam, J. "Racism," in *Dictionary of Mission Theology*, ed. John Corrie. Downers Grove: InterVarsity, 2007.

Manton, Thomas. *The Works of Thomas Manton*, 22 vols. Birmingham: Solid Ground Christian Books, 2008.

McClendon, Paul. *Paul's Spirituality in Galatians.* Eugene: Wipf & Stock, 2015.

McGrath, Alister E. *Christian Spirituality: An Introduction.* Oxford: Blackwell Publishers, 1999.

McKim, Donald K. *The Cambridge Companion to John Calvin.* Cambridge University Press, 2004.

Moisés, Silva. "Galatians" (pp. 785–812), in *Commentary on the New Testament Use of the Old Testament*, eds. G. K. Beale and D. A. Carson. Grand Rapids: Baker Academic, 2007.

Moore, Russell. *Adopted for Life: The Priority of Adoption for Christian Families and Churches.* Wheaton: Crossway, 2015.

Owen, John. *Communion with the Triune God*, eds. Kelly Kapic and Justin Taylor. 1657; Wheaton: Crossway, 2007.

Owen, John. *The Works of John Owen*, ed. W. H. Gould, 16 vols. London, 1850; rpt., Edinburgh: Banner of Truth, 1977.

Packer, J. I. *Knowing God.* London: Hodder and Stoughton, 1973.

Packer, J. I. *Serving the People of God*, in *The Collected Shorter Writings of J. I. Packer.* Carlisle: Paternoster, 2008.

Packer, J. I. "The Atonement in the Christian Life," in *In My Place Condemned He Stood: Celebrating the Glory of the Atonement*, eds. Mark Dever and J. I. Packer. Wheaton: Crossway, 2008.

Pate, Marvin. *The End of the Ages Has Come: The Theology of Paul*. Grand Rapids: Zondervan, 1995.

Perkins, William. *Commentary on Galatians*, in *The Works of William Perkins*, 10 vols. Grand Rapids: Reformation Heritage Books, 2015.

Piper, John. *The Future of Justification: A Response to N. T. Wright*. Wheaton: Crossway Books, 2007.

Piper, John. *The Satisfied Soul: Showing the Supremacy of God in All of Life*. New York: Multnomah, 2017.

Reeves, Michael. *Delighting in the Trinity: An Introduction to the Christian Faith*. Downers Grove: InterVarsity Press, 2012.

Sanders, Fred. *The Triune God*. Grand Rapids: Zondervan, 2016.

Schaeffer, Francis A. *True Spirituality*. Tyndale House Publishers, 1971.

Schaff, Philip (ed.). *The Creeds of Christendom*, 2 vols. Grand Rapids: Baker Books, 1998.

Schreiner, Thomas. *Galatians: Exegetical Commentary on the New Testament*. Grand Rapids: Zondervan, 2010.

Schreiner, Thomas. *The Law and Its Fulfillment: A Pauline Theology of Law*. Grand Rapids: Baker Books, 2001.

Sproul, R. C. *Loved by God*. Nashville: Word Publishing, 2001.

Stott, John R. W. *Baptism and Fullness*. London: Inter-Varsity, 1975.

Stott, John R. W. *The Message of Galatians*, in *The Bible Speaks Today*. Downers Grove: Inter-Varsity Press, 1968.

Swinnock, George. *The Works of George Swinnock*, ed. James Nichol, 5 vols. London, 1868; rpt., Edinburgh: Banner of Truth, 1992.

The Epistle of Mathetes to Diognetus, in *Ante-Nicene Fathers*, eds. Alexander Roberts & James Donaldson, 10 vols. Peabody: Hendrickson, 2004.

Thomas, I. D. E. (ed.). *A Golden Treasury*. Edinburgh: Banner of Truth, 2000.

Toon, Peter. *What is Spirituality? And is it for me?* London: Daybreak, 1989.

Watson, Thomas. *A Body of Divinity*. Edinburgh: Banner of Truth, 1958.

Wilcox, Thomas. *A Guide to Eternal Glory; or, Brief Directions to all Christians how to attain to Everlasting Life*. London, 1699.

Wright, N. T. *The New Testament and the People of God*. Minneapolis: Fortress, 1992.

Wright, N. T. *What Saint Paul Really Said: Was Saul of Tarsus the Real Founder of Christianity?* Grand Rapids: Eerdmans, 1997.

Yuille, J. Stephen. *A Hope Deferred: Adoption & the Fatherhood of God*. Wapwallopen: Shepherd Press, 2013.

Scripture Index

Old Testament

Genesis
- 1:28 139
- 1:31 156
- 2:25 78
- 3:5 129
- 3:7 78
- 3:15 .... 72, 74
- 3:21 78
- 4:5 143
- 8:21 8
- 12:2 72
- 12:3 66
- 13:16 72
- 15:5 72
- 15:6 66
- 17:4 66
- 17:7 72
- 17:8 81
- 17:14 34
- 17:19 74
- 18:18 66
- 21:10 111
- 21:12 74
- 22:17–18 72
- 26:4–5 72
- 28:14 72
- 37:8 143

Exodus
- 4:22 93
- 4:22–23 165
- 19:5 165
- 19:6 165
- 20:13 126
- 20:13–17 126
- 20:14 126
- 20:15 126
- 20:17 126
- 23:22 165
- 32:8 14

Leviticus
- 5:11 8
- 18:5 67
- 19:18 126

Numbers
- 8:8 8
- 25:11 25

Deuteronomy
- 1:31 93
- 4:35 90
- 6:3–5 126
- 6:4 90
- 6:4–6 112
- 7:6 165
- 8:5 93
- 10:12–13 126
- 14:1 165
- 14:2 165
- 21:23 68
- 27:26 67
- 28:58–60 67
- 32:15 165
- 33:12 165

Judges
- 6:22 144

1 Samuel
- 17:8–11 119
- 18:9 143

2 Samuel
- 7:12–14 74
- 6 46

1 Kings
- 4:21 81
- 7:15–22 25
- 8:27 97
- 19:10–14 25

1 Chronicles
- 16 46

Ezra
- 4:12–13 147

Esther
 5:9 143
Job
 11:7 90
Psalms
 15:1 46
 22:27–28 72
 24:3 46
 32:1–2 47
 32:3–4 150
 37:9 81
 37:11 81
 37:22 81
 37:29 81
 37:34 81
 47:7–9 72
 51:2 151
 69:9 127
 72:8–11 72
 86:10 90
 89:3–4 74
 93:2 90
 102:26–27 90
 103:13 93
 103:14 86
 119:68 156
 143:2 44
 145:3 89
 145:9 156
 147:3 ....149, 157
Proverbs
 4:23 150
 16:5 142
Isaiah
 1:2 165
 5:1–7 165
 6:5 144
 42:1 10
 44:2 165
 44:3 68

45:21 90
46:9 90
49:1–6 26
49:2 10
53:5 59
53:8 34
53:12 60
54:1 111
54:5–6 165
54:8–10 164
63:8 165
63:16 93
64:8 93
Jeremiah
 1:5 26
 3:19 93
 11:15 165
 11:19 34
 12:7 165
 12:10 165
 23:23–24 90
 31:31–33 125
 31:33 82
Ezekiel
 16:32 165
 36:25–27 61
 36:26–27 125
 36:27 68
Daniel
 6:3–4 144
Hosea
 1:2 165
 1:10 165
 11:1 165
Joel
 2:28 68
Habakkuk
 2:4 67
Zephaniah
 3:9–10 72

New Testament

Matthew
- 1:174
- 3:15 ... 44
- 4:2 ... 97
- 4:21 ... 147
- 5:3–6 ... 72
- 5:5 ... 81
- 6:26 ... 86
- 7:15 ... 17
- 7:23 ... 17
- 9:36 ... 97, 153
- 10:38 ... 51
- 11:28 ... 26, 149
- 11:28–31 ... 137
- 12:20 ... 137, 149
- 14:14 ... 97, 153
- 15:32 ... 97, 153
- 20:34 ... 97, 153
- 21:5 ... 137
- 22:37–38 ... 71
- 22:37–40 ... 126
- 25:23 ... 155
- 25:41–46 ... 136
- 26:37 ... 97

Mark
- 1:14 ... 95
- 1:15 ... 84
- 6:6 ... 97
- 7:21–23 ... 129
- 10:17 ... 74
- 10:21 ... 97
- 10:45 ... 86
- 12:30–31 ... 156
- 14:32–42 ... 97
- 15:34 ... 97

Luke
- 1:35 ... 97
- 2:52 ... 97
- 4:18 ... 157
- 5:32 ... 5
- 7:9 ... 97
- 7:48 ... 157
- 9:23 ... 51, 53
- 10:21 ... 137
- 12:50 ... 34
- 18:10–13 ... 119
- 18:40 ... 135
- 24:38–39 ... 97

John
- 1:1 ... 92
- 1:1–2 ... 95
- 1:12 ... 45
- 1:14 ... 91, 95, 97
- 1:14–16 ... 94
- 1:18 ... 91
- 1:29 ... 61, 78
- 1:33 ... 61
- 3:3 ... 124, 130
- 3:13 ... 99
- 3:16–18 ... 91
- 4:6 ... 97
- 5:23 ... 92
- 5:26 ... 89
- 5:30 ... 96
- 6:35 ... 45, 156, 157
- 6:37 ... 157
- 6:45 ... 26
- 7:37 ... 26
- 7:38 ... 157
- 8:12 ... 156, 157
- 8:42 ... 91, 96
- 8:56 ... 66
- 10:3 ... 103
- 10:10 ... 157
- 10:11 ... 157
- 10:14 ... 103
- 10:30 ... 91, 92
- 11:3 ... 97
- 11:33 ... 97
- 11:35 ... 97
- 11:38 ... 97
- 12:27 ... 97

Reference	Page
12:45	92
13:16	6
13:20	92
13:23	97
14:1	92, 135
14:6	156
14:7	92
14:9	92
14:10	92
14:16	135
14:16–17	91, 136
14:16–18	91
14:17	85, 94
14:23	94
14:26–27	91
14:27	137
15:1–5	165
15:9	137
15:11	97, 137
15:17	137
15:18-30	91
15:23	92
15:26	91, 96, 135
16:3	92
16:7	135, 136
16:7–15	91
16:32	92
17:1-26	91
17:2	103
17:3	44, 92
17:5	96
17:9	103
17:13	97
17:21–22	92
17:24	103
19:28	97
19:34	97
20:17	93
20:21	6
14:1	35

Acts
Reference	Page
2:38	61
7:34	9
7:38	73
7:53	73
9:26–30	24
10:15	32
11:27–30	24
11:29–30	34
12:11	9
13:47	109
13:49	6
14:4	6
14:21	6
15:24	16
16:3	26, 36
16:5	6
16:31	26
17:24–25	89
20:28	99
20:28–29	17
20:31	149
23:27	9
24:17	34

Romans
Reference	Page
1:4	51
1:6–7	26
1:8	14
1:18	103
1:18–32	102
1:19–20	103
1:29–32	80, 136
2:6–8	130
2:12–15	43
2:15	125
2:17–24	118
2:19–20	118
2:25–29	118
3:10	44
3:10–18	72
3:20	74
3:21	34, 36
3:21–26	34
3:24	94
3:25	68
3:27	119

3:28	119
4:7–8	47
4:13	81
4:19	111
4:25	18
5:1–2	7, 100
5:5	93
5:8	8
5:20–21	74
6:1–23	124
6:3	50
6:4	51
6:6	51, 124
6:7	51
7:7–8	74
7:9	26
7:18	144
7:19–24	136
8:1	42
8:2	133
8:3	8, 59, 98
8:3–4	112
8:6–8	124
8:8	18, 44
8:9	61, 85
8:11	61
8:12–13	132
8:13	62
8:17	85
8:23	81
8:25	86
8:26	85
8:28	69, 86
8:30	15
8:31–39	60
8:33–34	42
8:39	117
9:5	99
9:25	165
9:30–32	62
9:32	116
9:32-33	116
10:2	25

10:5	116
10:6-13	116
10:13	36, 47, 126
11:33	86, 89
12:2	53
13:9	126
13:10	126
13:12	9
14:1–3	80
14:19	127
15:2	125
15:17	34
16:17	17

1 Corinthians

1:3	93
1:4	14
1:9	11, 15
1:17–18	51
1:20	72
1:23	58, 119
1:26	15
1:30	78
2:2	58
2:7	23
2:8	99
2:10	23
2:13	148
2:15	148
3:1	148
3:9	165
3:21–23	69
6:9–10	136
6:19	61
7:17	156
7:29–31	9
8:4	90
8:6	93
9:11	148
9:20	35
9:21	35
9:22	35
10:11	9, 84
12:1	148

12:13 .... 61, 136
14:1 148
15:1 34
15:9 144
15:45 140

2 Corinthians
3:17 131
5:15 132
5:21 .... 13, 47, 97, 98, 153
8:1–15 34
8:3 6
9:1–5 34
9:15 107
11:2 165
11:3 57
11:24–27 165
12:9 100
12:11 144
13:4 51
13:14 94

Galatians
1:1-5 .... 5, 13, 14, 15, 41, 57, 123, 161
1:1-10 3
1:3 7
1:4 .... 7, 11, 52, 59, 117, 138, 162, 163
1:5 10
1:6 .... 14, 15
2:6 32
1:6-7 116
1:6-10 .... 13, 14, 41, 57, 123, 161
1:7 .... 15, 118, 119
1:8-9 17
1:11-2:14 .. 13, 21, 23, 25, 41, 57, 123, 161
1:11-12 .... 23, 33
1:11-15 32
1:11-24 .... 23, 32
1:13 25
1:13-2:14 24
1:13-15 24
1:13-24 25

1:14 25
1:15 15
1:15-16 25
1:16-24 .... 24, 32
1:23 28
1:24 27
2:1-10 .... 24, 32
2:1-11 33
2:1-14 .... 31, 32, 33
2:2 33
2:3 34
2:4 36
2:5 .... 32, 37
2:6 34
2:7-8 35
2:9 34
2:10 34
2:11 33
2:11-14 .... 25, 32
2:12 33
2:13 33
2:14 42
2:15 42
2:15-16 .... 42, 49
2:15-21 .. 14, 39, 41, 49, 57, 123, 161, 162
2:16 .... 42, 44
2:17-18 .... 42, 49
2:19-20 .... 42, 50
2:20 .... 50, 54, 138, 147
2:21 .... 42, 50
2:3-5 36
3:1 .... 58, 59
3:1-5 .... 57, 58, 101, 110, 116
3:1-5 66
3:1-5:12 .. 14, 41, 55, 57, 83, 123, 161
3:2 .... 58, 61, 66
3:3 .... 58, 61, 101, 110, 116
3:4 58
3:5 .... 59, 66
3:6-4:7 .... 58, 66, 101, 110
3:6-7 66

3:6-14 .... 65, 66, 84	4:8-20 .... 58, 101, 110, 116
3:8-9 66	4:9 102
3:9 163	4:9-20 104
3:10 .... 67, 136	4:11 104
3:10-11 43	4:12 104
3:11 67	4:12-14 104
3:12 67	4:13-6:10 14
3:13 .... 68, 97, 99, 116, 162	4:15 .... 58, 101, 110, 116
3:14 68	4:15-16 105
3:15 72	4:17-19 106
3:15-18 72	4:19 106
3:16 112	4:20 107
3:6-4:7 116	4:21 .... 58, 101, 110, 112, 116
3:15-26 71	4:21-31 .... 101, 109, 110
3:17 .... 72, 112	4:21-31 58
3:19 .... 73, 101	4:22 110
3:19-20 73	4:22-26 110
3:20 .... 90, 92	4:23 111
3:21 .... 58, 73, 101, 110, 116	4:24 111
3:21-26 73	4:25 111
3:22 136	4:26 111
3:22-23 73	4:27 111
3:24-25 73	4:28 .... 111, 112
3:25 136	4:28-31 111
3:26 165	4:29 111
3:27 .... 78, 163	4:31 .... 111, 112
3:27-4:7 .... 66, 84	5:1 .... 116, 128
3:27-29 77	5:1-12 .... 58, 101, 115
3:28 .... 35, 79, 163, 164	5:1-12 110
3:29 .... 81, 163, 164	5:2-3 117
4:1 84	5:2-4 117
4:1-2 84	5:4 .... 15, 117
4:1-7 83	5:4-6 117
4:2 84	5:5 117
4:3 .... 84, 136	5:6 .... 117, 119, 129
4:3-5 84	5:7 118
4:4 .... 10, 84, 90, 95, 112, 136	5:7-12 118
4:4-5 .... 44, 86	5:8 15
4:4-7 .... 89, 93	5:9-10 118
4:5 117	5:11 118
4:6 .... 61, 84, 90	5:12 119
4:6-7 85	5:13 .... 124, 128, 135
4:8 102	5:13-6:10 .... 41, 57, 121, 123, 161

5:13-15 123
5:13-16:10 123
5:14 .... 125, 147
5:15 .... 126, 135
5:16 .... 131, 155
5:16-17 .... 129, 135
5:16-24 51
5:17 .... 131, 137, 141, 142
5:18 .... 148, 155
5:18-25 135
5:19 .... 141, 155
5:19-21 136
5:20 147
5:20-21 142
5:21 136
5:22 .... 132, 140, 145, 153
5:22-23 .... 137, 155
5:23 149
5:24 138, 139, 144, 147, 153, 155
5:24-25 138
5:25 ...... 138, 141, 144, 148, 155
5:26 .... 141, 147, 155
6:1 .... 147, 148
6:1-5 147
6:1-10 155
6:2 147
6:2-5 149
6:3-5 150
6:6 154
6:6-10 153
6:7-8 154
6:9-10 155
6:10 153
6:11 161
6:11-17 .... 14, 41, 57, 123
6:11-18 161
6:11-17 161
6:12 162
6:12-14 162
6:13 162
6:14 162
6:15 164
6:15-16 163

6:16 164
6:17 165
6:18 ..... 14, 41, 57, 123, 161, 165
Ephesians
1:3 72, 94, 148
1:5 85
1:10 84
1:11 69
1:14 85
1:16 14
1:17 .... 23, 133
1:21 9
2:1 28
2:1–3 99
2:4–5 130
2:10 .... 154, 156
2:19 .... 155, 165
3:8 144
3:12 .... 86, 100
3:16–17 85
4:1 15
4:1–3 94
4:3 80
4:6 .... 89, 96
4:13 80
4:15–16 80
4:22–24 133
4:24 131
4:29–32 94
4:32 127
4:32–5:2 94
5:1–2 137
5:2 .... 8, 93
5:3–6 136
5:18–21 85
5:19 148
5:25–27 165
Philippians
1:3 14
2:3–4 .... 53, 80
2:6 96
2:7 96
2:13 133

2:25 6
3:2 17
3:4–6 162
3:6 27
3:7–8 162
3:18 .... 17, 51
3:21 81
4:19 100

Colossians
1:3 14
1:9 148
1:15–18 81
1:21 28
2:6–7 94
2:11 34
2:13 130
2:14 113
2:19 79
3:10 131
3:11 .... 79, 80
3:12 126
3:14 127
3:15 15
3:16 148

1 Thessalonians
1:214
1:4 ....
 165
1:9 102
2:7 149
2:13 7
4:7 15

2 Thessalonians
1:3 14
2:13 26
3:13 155

1 Timothy
1:5 117
1:13 27
1:14 27
1:15 144
1:16 27
2:5 .... 11, 90

2:6 9
2:6–7 99
4:6–16 154
5:3 154
5:17–18 154
6:1 154
6:12 15
6:15–16 96
6:18 154

2 Timothy
1:7 133
1:9 154
1:14 61
2:19 103
2:21 154
2:25 149
3:517

Titus
2:7 154
2:11–12 28
2:14 .... 9, 154, 165
2:11–12 137
3:1154
3:2 80
3:3 80
3:4 .... 137, 156
3:4–6 130
3:8 154
3:14 154

Philemon
1:18 65

Hebrews
2:2 73
3:1–2 137
4:15 .... 98, 100
4:16 100
5:8 137
7:25 99
7:26 98
8:10 130
9:14 98
9:22 78
9:24 100

10:26 8
11:3 29
11:9–10 81
12:1–2 51
12:2 .... 8, 97, 137
12:7 93
13:3 51
13:11 8

James
  2:14–26 154
  3:61 44
  3:14 142
  3:15 143
  3:16 143
  3:18 145
  5:11 149

1 Peter
  1:1–2 93
  1:3 93
  1:5 86
  2:5 148
  2:9 165
  2:11 142
  2:12 154
  2:16 124
  2:17 80
  2:22 98
  2:22–23 137
  3:18 .... 8, 18, 82

5:8 149

2 Peter
  1:3 133
  1:4 81
  3:9 137
  3:15 137

1 John
  1:3 93
  2:4 103
  3:1 93
  3:5 98
  3:6 103
  3:16 52
  4:8 92
  4:9 91
  4:9–10 94
  4:10 .... 8, 60

2 John
  1:10–11 17

3 John
  1:4 106

Jude
  1:3 23

Revelation
  1:6 165
  3:2 149
  3:17 75
  5:10 165
  22:12–16 136

www.ingramcontent.com/pod-product-compliance
Lightning Source LLC
Chambersburg PA
CBHW030038100526
44590CB00011B/247